Summoned and Shaped

Summoned and Shaped

Traveling Together into Our Belovedness

PAT HOFFMAN

Foreword by JIM MCDONALD

WIPF & STOCK · Eugene, Oregon

SUMMONED AND SHAPED
Traveling Together into Our Belovedness

Wipf & Stock
An Imprint of Wipf and Stock Publishers
199 W. 8th Ave., Suite 3
Eugene, OR 97401

www.wipfandstock.com

PAPERBACK ISBN: 978-1-5326-5448-0
HARDCOVER ISBN: 978-1-5326-5449-7
EBOOK ISBN: 978-1-5326-5450-3

Manufactured in the U.S.A.   NOVEMBER 7, 2018

Permissions to reprint:

Antonio Machado, Proverbs and Songs #29: ["Walker, your footsteps"] from Border of a Dream: Selected Poems, translated by Willis Barnstone. Copyright © 2004 by the Heirs of Antonio Machado. English translation copyright © 2004 by Willis Barnstone. Reprinted with the permission of The Permissions Company, Inc., on behalf of Copper Canyon Press, www.coppercanyonpress.org.

"The Process of Group Lectio" Chart 1, from Gathered in the Word, by Norvene Vest, published by Upper Room, copyright © Norvene Vest 1993.

Walker, your footsteps
are the road, and nothing more.
Walker, there is no road,
the road is made by walking.
Walking you make the road,
and turning to look behind
you see the path you never
again will step upon.
Walker, there is no road,
only foam trails on the sea.

Antonio Machado, "Proverbs and Songs #29"
translated by Willis Barnstone

Table of Contents

TABLE OF CONTENTS

Foreword

Back in 1981, Richard Bolles, the well-known author of *What Color is Your Parachute*, wrote a follow-up book called *The Three Boxes of Life and How to Get Out of Them*. It was, as the subtitle noted, an introduction to life/work planning. The three boxes Bolles identified were education, work, and retirement, and his point was that people tend to think of, and thus live, their lives as a straight-line movement through these three phases or boxes, with their clearly defined dimensions and expectations. He encouraged his readers not to be so linear or rigid about these aspects of living one's life, but instead to think and act creatively to balance the interplay between personal and professional growth, productivity and generativity, and recreation and leisure throughout one's life.

In some important ways, Pat Hoffman might not have been able to relate to Richard Bolles's book at all. As you will see in her moving and insightful story, Pat has never been in any of Bolles' three boxes. Her education was interrupted at twenty soon after she married her husband Cecil, a young seminarian at McCormick Seminary (later coming to San Francisco Theological Seminary). As a young married woman in the 1950s and sixties, her work life revolved around home, family, and church. If she had any thoughts about retirement they were tied to Cecil's vocational choices, not hers.

Reading Pat's story, one can see that Bolles's book seems more attuned to the male patterns of life, both then and now. The three boxes were more about the choices and mindsets of men rather than women. At the time Bolles wrote his book, women were just beginning to reenter the workforce in significant numbers after being pushed out at the end of World War II, encouraged by government-sponsored, male-dominated propaganda campaigns emphasizing women's place as being in the home, raising children, and supporting their husbands. Betty Friedan's 1963 book *The Feminine*

Mystique gave voice to the discontent of middle-class white women with this socially constructed order of things.

Pat never gave full assent to the social expectations of that time. Always present, bubbling up from deep within was her own restiveness and an insistent calling from the sacred spirit to a more expansive life in pursuit of compassion and justice. It's a powerful story she tells, and many will be able to relate to its dynamics, ups and downs, and drama.

The other aspect of Bolles's book was the idea that people should take control of their life and work by planning. Pat reveals to us the early psychological strictures that were placed on her ability to consciously plan. But we see, as she searches for a new work direction in mid-life, a way to do planning that is not attached to the outcome. We see her looking first for God's leading, and then, once she identifies a sense of direction, her intentionality and commitment to preparation, even knowing how slim her chances are in pursuit of the ministry she is pursuing. Along the way she is taken to new places internally and externally, confronting issues and circumstances that stretch her self-understanding and leave her dependent on God's grace. And yet, her lifelong attention to her own psychological, emotional, and spiritual growth as a human being commends her to people, who then entrust her with the responsibility to care for others who are struggling with life and death, addictions, and emotional and physical pain. This is a story of the importance of integrity and trustworthiness.

The convergence between Bolles's book and Pat Hoffman's *Summoned and Shaped* is the encouragement that both books offer with respect to how one gets out of the boxes of life that often confine us, whether they are of our own making or whether they are socially and externally imposed. Pat Hoffman found herself boxed in by her upbringing, by the church, and by society at large, and yet, by paying attention to the summons of God's sacred spirit, she overcame the boxes of her life. This book tells the story of a profound ministry of compassion, service, and justice for and with one of the most marginalized groups in American society. Her book not only chronicles how she navigated her struggle to claim this ministry, but it demonstrates how she herself was changed in small and large ways by that struggle and the ministry she pursued. It will make you laugh and cry, sometimes at the same time.

My wife, Dean, and I have known Pat and Cecil Hoffman since the summer of 1972, when Dean and I landed in Southern California to work for a year with the National Farm Worker Ministry. We had each finished one year of seminary and had married in June. Working for the NFWM as it supported the organizing efforts of Cesar Chavez and the United Farm Workers Union was an eye-opening experience for the two of us that profoundly altered our own lives and our understanding of ministry. As a member of the NFWM staff, Pat was one of the first people we met, and we immediately bonded. Over the course of our internship year, we had many occasions to break bread with Pat, Cecil, and their children, and they became mentors of sorts to this newlywed couple.

Over the next 46 years, we stayed in touch in various ways. Pat and I were both involved in the Sanctuary Movement for Central Americans during the 1980s and our paths crossed then. In the 1990s, Pat came to Washington, DC, where we then lived, when the AIDS Memorial Quilt was unfolded on the national mall for the first time as part of the NAMES Project, an encounter which is touched upon in this book. In 2011, when I became the president of San Francisco Theological Seminary, one of the first people I heard from was Pat, who reached out to congratulate me and offer words of encouragement as I began my tenure. Because we all now live in California, it has been easier for us to visit with each other on a more regular basis, a source of joy for us. In all this, one thing stands out: Pat Hoffman's deep, abiding commitment to show the love and justice of Jesus.

I wish I had had a book like this one when I was a seminarian. Pat never pursued ordination, but she also never let go of her summons to Christian ministry in its best, most authentic sense. In that sense, her story is a summons that any faith-centered person, ordained or otherwise, can take to heart and learn from. For those who are especially interested in chaplaincy, Pat's story can easily serve as a kind of model that illustrates the importance of self-reflection, vulnerability, and openness to the humanity of others—all of which are attributes that are foundational to the compassion and spiritual care that chaplaincy promises to provide for those who are suffering, confused, angry, or grieving. Whoever we are and wherever we are in life's journey, Pat's story will remind us afresh of the preciousness of life, the importance of courage and determination, the resilience of the human spirit, and the power of love to transform and shape us.

Jim McDonald
President and Professor of Faith and Public Life
San Francisco Theological Seminary
San Anselmo, CA

July 20, 2018

Preface

These are stories from one period in my life and a chaotic period in the lives of people in the AIDS-affected community. I hope you'll experience these as sacred stories, stories which I hope may inspire you, touch you, and help you hear God speaking to you. I would be thrilled if these stories somehow amplify the voice of God speaking to you from some suffering community, "Here I am, here I am."

In Isaiah 58, the people felt God's absence from the nation. God told them to get busy, rebuild the ancient ruins, and to be repairers of the breach and restorers of ruined neighborhoods. It was God's will to reclaim the community's safety and dignity. Those complaining were instructed to engage themselves in restorative work.

After you read *Summoned and Shaped*, I hope you will notice events, encounters, or stories in the news that stay on your mind, and will notice if particular people whom you may not know are calling to you in their suffering. Allow yourself to believe that just as in Isaiah 65, when God was calling to the people of that time, God may now be calling to you. "Here I am, here I am," says Yahweh, extending a hand toward the people passing by. Where are you seeing God's face? How will you respond? We can't take on everything that calls to us, except in small ways and in prayer. Yet, we need to notice if some call has our name on it. If it occurs for you, don't hesitate to respond to the summons and let God's Spirit shape you by deep engagement with people struggling for justice. And if some approach I used will help in the work you do I would treasure, in that way, being one of your companions.

Pat Hoffman

Acknowledgements

Did anyone ever have more brilliant readers/critiquers than I have had? I lift them up here: the Rev. Chris Hartmire, long-time friend, former Director of the National Farm Worker Ministry and my mentor in an immersive style of ministry; the Rev. Chris Glaser, my friend and fellow writer, guide into a community where I was allowed to serve; Art McDermott, M.A., my friend and fund developer extraodinaire who noticed what was missing in the manuscript as well as what was there, and has lived this story; the Rev. Dr. James McDonald, an old friend and leader in Christian justice work who wedged reading the manuscript into an enormously busy schedule as President of San Francisco Theological Seminary; my husband, the Rev. Dr. Cecil Hoffman, who is one of the most literate people I know, and is always so gentle when I lay a new-born manuscript in his lap; my daughter Mary Hoffman, M.A., contemplative and healer, who has a deep understanding of my work, and a deep kindness. Two others who read early versions of the book were my daughter Ruth Cooper, MFT, who has cheered me on; and my friend and neighbor, the Rev. Dr. Joyce DeGraaff, who helped me see how I presented myself in the early version. Words are inadequate to express my gratitude for their guidance and encouragement.

The patients and clients I write about have been foundational in this story. Those who have died and those living are held here in sacred memory. I have changed their names in the book with the exception of those who were able to give me permission to use their names.

1

Searching

Ihad been laid up for months as I moved into my fifties. There were two knee surgeries when I was fifty-one. In each case, for a month afterward I couldn't walk down the hill in front of our house to the sidewalk, and I wasn't supposed to drive. I put off a recommended hysterectomy. But after I was in St. Louis for work in the summer I knew it was time.

I had taken all white clothes. Lovely for summer. Not so good for a woman with an iffy uterus. I was at the Presbyterian General Assembly promoting my book, *Ministry of the Dispossessed: Learning from the Farm Worker Movement,* and was to attend a big breakfast meeting, sitting at the head table with Cesar Chavez, President of the United Farm Workers. I remember being sick as a dog from the little no-bleed pills I had started taking the day before. When I returned to Los Angeles, I scheduled the hysterectomy for July 6, the day after my 54th birthday.

I wasn't used to being sidelined. I did my best to take charge of my time following these surgeries, but feelings of helplessness were undeniably present. I remember thinking, "You know, Pat, these downtimes are likely to increase as you get older. I think you have some issues here."

I had been attracted to empowerment work in the past, in the form of the farm worker movement, where I spent five years on the staff of the National Farm Worker Ministry (NFWM), organizing and writing about Cesar Chavez's now-famous movement of the seventies and eighties. It had been the perfect job for me at the time, giving me a chance to join an effective movement for change and to have some challenging opportunities for my own development. The job included frequent travel on my own, leading actions and trainings for church-based supporters, and writing articles for denominational magazines with a director, the Rev. Chris Hartmire, who had respect for women's abilities—rather a rarity at that time.

Chris seemed confident in my abilities, and frankly was too busy getting denominations on board in support of the UFW to worry about whether I might miss my planes or screw up my assignments. And I didn't. My experience of his confidence freed me to do things that others during the seventies would never have expected me to do. After I left the NFWM, I continued my relationship with the farm workers for fifteen more years, writing articles and a book about the movement.

I went on to do other social justice work. Being an agent for change was significant to my sense of myself. ✓ Change Agent

By the time I hit fifty-four, I was coming to terms with the limits of that identity and knew I needed to notice what was driving my need to participate in social change movements. I needed to tease out the prophetic impulse from my personal need to feel enabled. I remember having a dream around that time, one that consisted entirely of a huge, see-through Plexiglass board with the verb *poder* conjugated on it (*poder* means "to be able"). The UFW's call to action, later picked up by Barack Obama's campaign, was "*Si, se puede.*" "We are able."

God was calling me to examine what it meant to feel "able." I had poured myself into being an agent for just change. The dream was telling me there was a shadow side to my social action life which I needed to see and own. I knew I needed to make changes in my life, but did not know what needed to change, or how I would go about making the necessary change. I was like a sailboat caught in a vast calm with no wind to move me in any direction. I didn't even know what direction I wanted or needed to go in.

I had some "learned helplessness" from being raised in a family which discouraged independent action. My sister and I experienced a lot of obstacles to healthy self-development. I remember when I was in my late twenties, I was at my parents' home working with my Dad in their garage, helping them pack for a move to Palm Springs. Suddenly, unexpectedly, he burst out with an angry accusation that I liked farm workers better than him and Mother. I was stunned and deeply hurt. This kind of angry retribution created anxiety about following my heart. But I had decided that anxiety and passivity would not write my story.

In my life I have encountered obstacles, but also encouragements. The encouragements have operated in my more conscious mind, enabling me to make "I can do this" decisions. The obstacles created underlying anxiety related to many endeavors and often kept me from fully owning my abilities. I envy friends who talk about their father or mother or some continuing person in their early life who believed in them. That must be sweet.

One of my life's projects is looking for what benefit can be gleaned from the absence of that person. Now God was calling me to another project: to look through to the deeper meanings of *poder*. I had learned about making change. How might I sit with things as they were? Could that possibly constitute power? Could that make a contribution to a world in need?

2

Finding a New Direction

Relationships which alter our lives can begin routinely. When did I first get involved with the gay community? I'm not sure. But I'm pretty sure it began with Chris Glaser. He was in his twenties and was a recent graduate of Yale Divinity School. He came into our presbytery to develop the Lazarus Project at West Hollywood Presbyterian Church, where the Rev. Ross Greek was pastor. His job was to minister to LGBT adults, helping them reconnect with their Christian faith, and helping straight folks, including parents, understand the gay and lesbian experience.

When Chris came into our presbytery he was a candidate for the ministry. He wasn't the first openly gay candidate, but became the candidate around whom a national debate over ordination of gays and lesbians swirled for years. We got to know each other in relationship to this and other social issues. I served on peace and justice committees for the presbytery. When I was working on a justice resolution, I could always count on Chris's support.

In 1984, I remember spotting him sitting alone in the back of a large, rather dark sanctuary during a boring part of a presbytery meeting. I slipped into the pew beside him and whispered, "Would you like to go to Nicaragua?" "Yes," he said with his Irish humor, "can we go now?" He and I became part of a group of twenty that spent a week in Nicaragua during that country's first democratic election.

That whole week was amazing, but I'm not going down that road right now. What I am especially remembering was the bonding Chris and I experienced. On the long plane trip from L. A. to Nicaragua, we were seatmates, and, at my request, he took those hours to tell me his whole story of growing up in a deeply religious household, then in school meeting the reality that he was gay, struggling to come to terms with that as a Christian, going to seminary, seeking ordination, and now hitting all these roadblocks to ministry.

Chris's story of the church's non-acceptance of who he was has resonance with the stories of many gays and lesbians, and it connected with me as a woman. Growing up, struggling to be seen for who I was prepared my heart to hear Chris's story. I was also aware that the details in the church's fight over gay ordination (picking a few passages from the Old Testament to support what was essentially a societal bias) were the same as the church had used twenty years earlier over women's ordination. The exact same playbook, just a different set of Scriptures.

A couple years later, Chris was writing his first book, *Uncommon Calling*, (he's now published twelve with a new one in the works) while I was writing mine about the farmworker movement, *Ministry of the Dispossessed*. We started getting together regularly for coffee, sometimes splurging on scones. We would read each other's chapters and talk about them. I would usually drive up to West Hollywood. Every visit became another hour or two of my being tutored in Gay Culture 101. I may even have moved into Gay Culture 201. Chris has a great, earthy sense of humor. We'd be walking along Santa Monica Boulevard toward the restaurant, and he'd see a man he knew from his church and say, "See that guy. I'd introduce you to him but he's busy cruising that truck driver."

My husband Cecil, a Presbyterian clergyman, and I enjoyed a friendship with Chris and his partner George, another seminary-trained man, who was doing secular work. Cecil and I were guests at their home for dinner. They came with us and another couple to the Hollywood Bowl for a picnic and concert for my birthday. Being with gay people became part of my reality, part of my life. I joined the Board of the Lazarus Project at the West Hollywood Church where I got to know more gay men and widened my friendships with lesbians.

The impact of AIDS on the gay community often came up as Chris and I met for coffee. The epidemic had hit hard in West Hollywood, with its large gay population. Every week, people in West Hollywood were getting the shocking news that another friend or partner was sick and had learned they had HIV/AIDS.

AIDS had not yet touched me in a personal way, but it was a huge reality for Chris, accentuated after Ross Greek retired and Chris became the *de facto* pastor of what was by then a mainly gay and lesbian congregation.

Cecil saw me floundering about where to go with my work life. I had accepted a variety of short-term work assignments. In the meantime, I was thinking about getting a Master's degree and looked into sociology or anthropology. Nothing seemed like a good fit. Cecil suggested I try volunteering in order to get an idea about some new career path. Because of my friendship with Chris, AIDS Project Los Angeles (APLA) came to mind. I contacted them and learned they had an immediate need for a hospital visitor on a newly dedicated AIDS unit at Daniel Freeman Marina Hospital, just a few miles from our home in North Inglewood. I hesitated to take a position at a hospital. I didn't like hospitals. I had recently had those surgeries and hospitals made me anxious. I felt like I lost power in hospitals. I told APLA I wanted to lead small support groups, but they said they only used licensed psychotherapists for those positions. So I signed on for the hospital visitor job and registered for their training.

3

Exploring Hospital Visitation

I began this challenging new venture in May 1989. I felt uncomfortable in the hospital setting at first and had to learn everything: how to tell a floor nurse from a nurse manager, the geography of the place, how things were done, what the different codes meant that were announced by overhead page, and to stay out of the way during a Code Blue.

However, I felt comfortable with the patients I was visiting: all men at that time, and all gay. I was like a woman who had received culture and language training for foreign service. In the normal course of our years of friendship, I had absorbed so much from Chris about gay culture, so I felt at home visiting the patients, asking them about their lives, their families, their lovers.

I visited on Tuesday and Thursday afternoons. In the mornings I worked at a mental health clinic in an administrative position to bring in a little money. Much of the rest of the time my mind and heart were engaged with the patients I was meeting. And I was searching for how to be with these men who were soon going to die.

In my work with the farmworkers I had felt strong and empowered by them. They had built a movement and I was part of it, swept along by their savvy, their determination, and their program. I was aware that my sense of identity and value had been wrapped up with their movement. I remember once going with Cecil to an alumni day at Occidental College. I wore my United Farm Worker button because it helped me feel like I knew who I was. "I'm an activist and part of a movement that is making significant social change."

Because of my shaky identity as a young woman, I could be a little brittle at times. I remember in about 1971, after I was on staff with the NFWM, friends from church invited us to their home for a small dinner party. Cecil and I did not know the other guests. I was seated next to a man who taught somewhere. He turned to me asking, "Are you just a—?" Before he could get "housewife" out of his mouth I said, "No I'm not a 'just a.' I'm on the staff of the National Farm Worker Ministry." My response was entirely lacking in kindness. It told me, however, how sick I was of that particular question, which I found demeaning. "Are you a homemaker?" would have been acceptable. Better yet would have been, "Pat, tell me about yourself."

I've been rereading the journal I kept for the year and a half when I was an APLA hospital visitor. I can see how I was struggling with identity. Who was I, sitting quietly at the bedside of men who were ill with a little-understood virus, men the age of my children, moving inexorably toward death? If I was still an agent of change, I could not recognize how. My journal note soon after I started reads, "It's only a week and a half since I began and already I feel shaky inside and terribly vulnerable." The deaths of the patients, one died the first week and another the second, shook my weak sense of self, which had been shored up by my identification with the effectiveness of the farm worker movement.

I remember being on a walk with Cecil in our neighborhood. I was telling him how fragile I felt. I was surprised by his response, "That's good." he said, "That means some old ways of coping are breaking down leaving room for growth."

His response underscored what I was beginning to understand. I needed to find a more reliable source of strength and identity rooted in my own center, from a source found within me.

Bryle, the Unit Nurse Manager, took me around the unit on the first day to introduce me to some of the patients. Tom was one of the first men I met. I never would have guessed he had been an athlete, a professional ice skater. AIDS was ravaging his body. I would visit him regularly, but occasionally he would be discharged. On June 7th, I wrote:

> When I got to the hospital yesterday, I found that Tom had been discharged. The lack of closure or continuity with patients is hard for me. I wanted another conversation. I wanted to be in touch.

8

"How are you doing, Tom? How is it to be home?" But for now, at least, there is a terminus in that relationship.

I'm trying to learn how to handle these—I don't even know what to call them—"hospital friendships." I'm trying to learn how to be all there as authentically as I can for a few minutes, for a few times, and to let go of anything further…I'm trying to let go of problem solving and let go of "being there" for people in some ongoing way. It's hard.

It may be a more realistic way of living in the world, to be present as fully as possible in the moments life presents and then to let go and let the love and care we share do its own work. We can change so little in a lifetime. I'm learning some lessons in limits.[1]

The second week in June, I was making a second visit to Michael, an APLA client. He was feeling miserable and a little lonely. He asked if I could find him an APLA buddy. The buddy program lined up specially trained volunteers to visit clients. I said I would check about it. I wondered if I should be encouraging him to check for himself, but I didn't mention that. In my journal I wrote:

Following through on patient requests restores in me a sense of control and usefulness. It's my turtle shell to keep me from feeling soft and exposed to the "predators." And what are they? The anxiety of being myself without a role? The experience of being present to suffering and unable to "help?" The knowledge of my own finitude?[2]

Later in June, I had my first visit to the Intensive Care Unit (ICU). I was in the hallway of the AIDS unit talking with Byrle when Tom's partner, Robert, hurried toward us. He asked me if I had seen Tom and I told him, "No, is he in the hospital?" He said yes, in the ICU, and then he asked where it was. I didn't know. But Byrle, with a sense of efficient urgency, said he would walk with us to ICU, that he would have to take us in.

We reached the double doors for ICU opening off the hallway… Byrle swept us into a restricted corridor for a short distance. At the door to ICU he told us to wait. He stepped in and found which cubicle Tom was in and then returned to direct us…

Tom, a gnarled head muzzled with a blue oxygen mask. A rasping, frantic sound of breathing. Where was his body? There was scarcely a shape visible under the sheet. It was as though his

1. Hoffman, *AIDS and the Sleeping Church*, 16.
2. Hoffman, *AIDS and the Sleeping Church*, 21.

body had disappeared and left only his head. I moved closer, Robert on his right and I on his left. I could see a little of his anguished face above the mask. He spoke to Robert with urgency. First a status report. "They are trying to regulate my breathing." Then "Did you speak to my father?" Robert responded yes. "Did you talk about the insurance?" I missed Robert's response, so overwhelmed was I by what I was experiencing. Tom's face had been turned toward me as he spoke to Robert as though it would take too much precious energy to both turn and speak. Without lifting his head he raised his eyes. "Is it Kay?" he asked me, making an effort to remember my name. "Pat. That's all right," I reassured him.

"I need a towel," Tom said with urgency. "And I need it now." Byrle was at the end of the bed and grabbed a towel from a table I had not noticed. "I need it under me." Byrle deftly smoothed the towel under him managing to keep Tom's emaciated body covered. I was impressed with the control and dignity Tom was able to manage under the circumstances.

Robert was caressing Tom's arms as they lay under the cover, just as I had seen him do the first time I met them. I found Tom's shoulder to touch it. Then in a wave of feeling I stroked his forehead. Tom was not the kind of man to invite such a show of affection, but it was so near the end. "Dear friend," I said to him, and tears seemed to well up in his eyes. "I'm not going to stay." So much was happening and Tom had urgent matters to settle with Robert. I felt out of place. I started for the door, but saw Robert break into tears and turn away from Tom. So Tom wouldn't see? I went around the bed and embraced Robert, kissed his face.

I didn't see Byrle as I went through the door, although he must have been standing right there. I wasn't crying. I simply did not have the capacity to take in anything else. Then I saw that Byrle was right behind me, leaving with me. We went through the door and down the corridor toward the double doors.

When we got through the double doors, Byrle told me what he was going to do. What he said didn't entirely register and I was surprised that he would be telling me. I couldn't think of why … Maybe he was upset too and this was a way to get closure on the experience we had just had together.[3]

The things he told me were routine things like, "I'm going back to my office and then I'm going to check on a new patient."

---

3. Hoffman, *AIDS and the Sleeping Church*, 29, 30.

It was the end of the day for me. I left the hospital and drove home, pondering this intense experience and hoping what I had said and done, and my leaving to give Tom and Robert privacy, had been appropriate. Such access to personal suffering was new territory for me. After an hour of stewing at home, I phoned Bryle and just asked him, had my leaving been the right thing to do? He assured me it had been exactly right. Tom died ten days later in the evening, with Robert by his side.

In mid-July, Robert hosted a memorial occasion for Tom at the apartment they had shared. He invited me. It was the first of many memorials I would attend for people who had died of AIDS, but it is memorable for me in a specific way. After a time for the guests to socialize, Robert stood up in the middle of the room with a plastic flute of champagne in one hand and a greeting card in the other. He told us the message seemed to fit how Tommy would want to be remembered, and then he read it, his hands shaking hard. But he got through it and raised his glass in a toast to Tommy. In that moment, and before the well-planned eulogies, I could remember other memorial services, conducted by clergy who were there to assist and support the bereaved, leading the service so the bereaved could grieve, a little out of the spotlight. Where are the clergy, I wondered? And where are the church's gifts of comforting liturgies in this time of devastation of our country's gay community? It was at that moment that a kernel of intention began to form in me out of both love and anger: perhaps I could help open the storehouse of what the institutional church at its best could offer to this suffering community: hope-giving sacred stories, prayers, and spiritual practices which can guide and support us.

One Tuesday, Dr. Murray, an infectious disease specialist who frequently saw patients in Unit 500, asked me to accompany her for a family consultation. I had not met the patient, who had arrived on the Unit since my last visit the prior Thursday. Like many, his new AIDS diagnosis would be the first time the family knew, or acknowledged, that this son or brother was gay.

When the family was assembled around the bedside, Dr. Murray and I joined them and introduced ourselves. Then Dr. Murray explained in detail the patient's medical condition. When she was finished she asked if family members had questions. They seemed stunned. How much of this could they even take in? They managed a few requests for clarification, but their surprise and sorrow at the diagnosis must surely have drowned any immediate ability for rational thought.

Dr. Murray then excused herself. I had not had time to consider what my role would be. Had Dr. Murray suggested to the patient that the APLA volunteer could be there to support him or to help the family? Perhaps she understood that someone needed to help them in that earth-shaking encounter. I stayed with them for a little while.

Dr. Murray was asking me to act at a capacity I wasn't aware of having; a capacity I was able then to live into. I was grateful she had invited me to be there, supporting a gay man in his experience of being outed by AIDS. Dr. Murray's view of me was in my encouragement column.

4

A Loss I had Buried

My sister Martha, fellow struggler in the search for self, had taken her own life in 1968, at age 39. She had been living near my parents in Palm Springs. Her death had been a devastating blow to me. That loss came back to me like a stealth bomb. It happened in relationship to Mark, a patient I was getting to know.

When I started on the Unit, Mark didn't seem as sick as some of the others. But he was arriving at, and leaving, the hospital often. In fact, this happened three times in my first month. Mark and I hit it off from the beginning. He was outgoing and liked company. One day he was pretty sick, hooked up to an IV and flat on his back. We visited a while and when I was needing to go I asked him if there was anything I could do for him, a question I didn't normally ask. He looked at me and said, "No, just be you."

"Just be you." I was struck by this simple statement, like it was an idea no one had ever suggested to me before. Maybe no one had. I didn't have to be maternal, didn't have to be useful, didn't have to be making social change. I could just be me. For Mark that was sufficient. An astonishing gift.

In July, Mark was back in the hospital and having a hard time of it. He had a parasite that had almost killed him the previous year. He felt miserable, and his partner was down with the flu, so he couldn't visit. Mark was feeling angry at almost everyone, but he welcomed my visit, during which he expressed all the lousy things that had been happening. That visit went into my journal.

I sat and listened. When I was ready to go I asked: "Would you like a hug, Mark?" "I sure would." We hugged and then he said, "Today started out rotten, but it's getting better." That made me feel marvelous...

It's hard to believe that our best gift might be to sit and wait, through the pauses when nothing is said, through the anger, and sometimes through the abrupt responses. All my life I have believed that the mark of caring was the willingness to do something, to take action, to be an advocate. Now I see that there is also a place for caring of another kind. A tree does nothing, but we love its shade. We can stretch out our arms like leafy branches and bring coolness and shade in the desert.[1]

Three days later, Mark specifically asked for me to come talk with him. He had decided to "let go." His plan was to stop eating and stop his medications. He had spoken with his mother, his lover, his sister, and his close friend, Carol. They had all given him permission. Now, to my astonishment, he was asking for my permission. It was not a step I was emotionally prepared to take, which I told him. I said I would think about it and would be back.

For three days I was in inexplicable distress over Mark's wish to end his life. I was aware I was more upset than this relationship could explain. The night of the third day I prayed God would send me a dream to help me understand what was happening. The dream that came to me was such a gift. It was a dream about my sister, who had been just Mark's age when she took her own life some twenty years earlier.

In the 1960s when Martha died, our society paid little attention to grief care. The weekend after Martha's funeral, Cecil was to help staff a church youth camp in the mountains. My close friend, Louise Jongewaard, came to spend that night with me. God bless her. For the most part, people seemed just to expect me to get over it and move on with life. What happened for me was the grief went underground and only surfaced now and then. I realized it had surfaced in disguise when Mark told me he wanted to "self-deliver."

The next day I went to see Mark and told him about my dream and thanked him for sharing at a level that helped my unresolved grief to surface. He was tearful and then began to ask me questions.

1. Hoffman, *AIDS and the Sleeping Church*, 38.

We were having a real conversation. It had been so easy for me before. I had been like a computer tutor. Whatever Mark inputted was received and I printed out supportive messages. But love and struggle had burst me out of my one-dimensional form. Mark was challenging me and forcing me to be authentic.[2]

When I was finished, Mark shared with me that he had spoken with his doctor, who had convinced him that his plan to stop meds and eating would not result in him dying in a week, as he had hoped. He could go off his medications for a while and there was no reason for him not to go home. Mark had decided that's what he wanted to do.

When I told Mark I needed to go, he held out his arms to give me a hug. This time it was me receiving comfort. I was not a pleasant, supportive hologram in the room. I was a person, interacting. At a deeper level than I could understand at that time, my real self was coming into view, both for me and for those I was meeting.

2. Hoffman, *AIDS and the Sleeping Church*, 45.

5

My First Formal Job Interview: Success!

Ten months into this volunteer work I knew I wanted to be working in the AIDS-affected community, but in what kind of position was unclear. I was working now a few hours a week as the editor of a monthly newsletter for the Southern California Interfaith AIDS Coalition and was attending their meetings at Good Samaritan Hospital in downtown Los Angeles, but I was looking for more than that.

It was a Sunday in early February. I was lingering at the breakfast table with the *Los Angeles Times,* and I turned to the classified section. California State University, Long Beach (CSULB) was advertising four AIDS-related positions at their Research and Education Project on that campus. The first three were not a fit for me, but the fourth seemed like a possibility, and it was half-time, which suited me. The position was for an Assistant Program Coordinator, who would be responsible for the coordination of educational seminars for health care professionals and the development of training curriculum. As the ad read, it required a Master's Degree in applied behavioral science or equivalent and they were looking for experience in health education/community education and finally, familiarity with WordPerfect 5.0. It gave the address for applying. (This was two or three years before the start of the internet and ubiquitous email.)

I phoned an old friend, Rev. Jim White, the campus pastor at CSULB and asked if he would check out this project and let me know what he found. Two days later he wrote me with details on the Project. He had found no red flags. With this, I felt ready to proceed.

My prayer life at that time was in transition. Looking back, my fervent prayer was expressed in the full attention I gave to my heart's message to try for this job. Looking back now on the resume I crafted, I can only imagine the gumption it took for me to present myself as one who did not have a Master's Degree, but who had conducted training programs and had written curriculum. And in order for my resume to reflect AIDS involvement, I listed "AIDS Project Los Angeles Hospital Liaison," with my duties. The next section I listed was my writing, and at the top of that was, "Writing book based on hospital visitation with PWA's" (People With AIDS, the gay community's preferred terminology at the time). On the back side of the resume, the first item under Publications was "An AIDS Journal, in preparation." At that time I was scarcely mentioning the journal to anyone. I did know in my heart that I intended it for publication, but it was so different from anything else I had published. It felt like such a reach that I didn't want to mention it to friends or colleagues and set myself up for embarrassment if they started asking how the book was coming along and if I had a publisher for it. But there it was, featured prominently on my resume. I wanted this job and I wanted to look like a person who could produce for them.

Also, I had never used WordPerfect, so before I wrote the application letter, I went to the computer store and bought a WordPerfect 5.0 manual and skimmed through it. Cecil and I were among the early adopters of personal computers and I was well acquainted with a devilishly difficult program called WordStar, so having learned that one, I reasoned that I could learn a newer program. In the application letter I stated, "I am familiar with WordPerfect 5.0." I was nervous saying that, however the whole application seemed such a stretch that I decided, "What the heck, I'm going for it."

They called me to come in for an interview! Most of my work experiences had been with people I knew, with friends, or friends of friends. I was fifty-four years old and this was my first formal job interview. It had taken chutzpah for me to write the resume, now I had to present the person I had written about.

I don't know if the interview went well. I guess it went well enough, or maybe I was the only applicant, but by mid-March I received a letter confirming my "appointment as Assistant Program Coordinator with the AIDS Research & Education Project." My immediate supervisor would be Gary Humfleet, PhD. Gary, a young clinical psychologist, was one of several people who had interviewed me.

The weekend before I started the job I took a crash course on WordPerfect 5.0. I was as ready as I was going to be.

There were fourteen staff, many of them young graduate students, and were predominantly gay men. The staff was very busy but always helpful to me. This was easily the most high-tech site I had worked in. Each cubicle had a computer and they were networked and everyone used one printer. I also was introduced to the use of a FAX machine. A female administrative assistant taught me to fax, but there were so many sides and portals that when I tried to use it a day or two later, I put the pages to fax in a receiving portal then wondered why it wouldn't send. I think I had to ask her twice more to instruct me. That was embarrassing.

Gary and I shared a small office with my desk facing one wall and his another. I think we shared a computer, which was on its own table facing a third wall. On each wall were large safe sex posters showing hunky, naked men having sex or intending to have sex. I did not have the impression that these were displayed as a reminder to staff to practice safe sex. One poster was directly in front of me each work day.

Gary had had a practice in child psychology. He told me that when the AIDS crisis struck, he left his practice and came to California to help his community. Gary had little wind-up toys covering almost every inch of his desk, a reminder, perhaps, of his earlier profession. He had a relaxed way about him, which I enjoyed.

Gary had me join him on a team which planned and conducted trainings for health care workers. When I joined the team there was one other woman and the rest were gay men. It was a very smart, fun group to work with. I had worked with straight men for years and this was definitely more relaxing. What was it about it that I liked? I was just one of the group. I felt I could be myself. I remember one day I arrived at our meeting in a conference room where we were seated around a large conference table. I took out the notes I'd made at home about a training we were going to plan. I'd written the notes on a piece of heavy white paper that was the liner from a package of nylon stockings. One of the men spotted that and said, "I recognize that paper. I've had some of my best experiences with those" (meaning the nylons). I felt right at home. It was okay to be a woman. It was okay to bring my notes on the stocking liner. And I could enjoy some gay humor. I was among friends.

My time was only partly utilized by these health and mental health worker trainings, so one day I asked Gary what his most pressing need was. He said they were in the second year of a three-year grant from the

National Institute of Mental Health (NIMH) to train physicians in mental health issues and HIV/AIDS. So far they had not trained a single physician. I offered to do some research to get ideas about how the project might reach physicians. He encouraged me to go ahead.

I started phoning some of the big disease organizations like the American Heart Association. They all told me the same thing, that doctors are required to get Continuing Medical Education units each year and that one way they got them was to go to free lunches these organizations put on at · local hospitals with speakers. The doctors got their lunch, saw their friends, and got CMEs. I proposed this approach to Gary and he liked it, but said he didn't think physicians would come out to hear anyone but a doctor, or maybe a lawyer, if they needed to protect themselves from lawsuits. He put me in charge of seeing how we might implement such a program to fulfill the requirements of the mental health grant.

I contacted Dr. Patricia Murray, Dr. Michael Murphy, and Dr. Stephen Gabin, whom I had gotten to know at Daniel Freeman Marina Hospital, where I continued to visit patients in the evenings. They were interested in preparing more doctors to be informed about, and to work with, the epidemic.

The doctors and I and Mark Senak, a lawyer whose partner had died of AIDS, got together for breakfast at a hotel near LAX (I think this was the first breakfast meeting I'd ever planned) to discuss presentations they might make about the treatment of AIDS that could include some psychosocial/mental health features. They all seemed enthusiastic about doing this outreach. Doctors who were treating AIDS patients were frustrated by how few of their fellow physicians were educating themselves so they could recognize symptoms in their patients. Unfortunately, many physicians were not aware that they might be treating gay men and were not yet thinking that non-gay men and women could also become infected. Doctors were known to say, "I don't need HIV/AIDS education because I don't have any of those people in my practice."

At our breakfast meeting, we came up with ways for each to include psychosocial material in presentations that were otherwise about diagnosing and treating HIV/AIDS, from the perspective of each presenter's specialty. Mark, the attorney, was looking forward to letting physicians know the possible legal challenges if they ignored HIV/AIDS symptoms in their patients. The AIDS Research and Education staff gave me names of additional people in Long Beach who joined the panel: Dr. Audra Deveikas, a specialist in pediatric AIDS, and Dr. Dan Martin, a psychiatrist.

These core members of the panel now needed to write outlines and objectives so our staff could prepare pre- and post-tests for each of their presentations. I also needed to compile a list of hospitals, primarily in the city of Long Beach, with the names of staff responsible for their continuing education luncheons.

One day during this period, the director of our Research and Education Project came into our little office. Gary and I were both there, but he had come to speak to me. Tall and lanky, he pulled out the computer chair. I turned my chair around to face him. Gary turned to be part of the circle but was just listening. The director gave me a talking-to about getting this program going (the program that had trained no physicians during the year before I was hired). When he was finished he said, "I'm trying to jack you up." "I don't need jacking up," I responded. The director probably was worried about the National Institute of Mental Health grant that they had not yet been able to perform on. Thinking back on this encounter I'm surprised how unintimidated I was. All the incentive I needed was already in my heart from the patients I'd gotten to know and care about, and say goodbye to.

We had lift-off for the Physician Education Program in late July 1990. I had marketed our speakers as a series and tried to schedule each one of them separately at each hospital in the Long Beach area. Our staff worked with me to prepare the pre- and post-tests for each speaker's presentation. Over the next eight months we had fifteen presentations in eight hospitals to more than four hundred physicians, most of whom probably had never before gotten any continuing medical education related to HIV/AIDS. With the help of our program staff, I had developed a way to do this. It was fueled by commitment to patients I had met at Marina Hospital. I didn't have a Master's degree, but I brought relationships, some inventiveness, and hard work to this effort to chip away at the stigma surrounding AIDS.

In 1990, I needed to give up visiting patients at Marina Hospital. It had been a year and a half of privileged conversations as I had gotten to know patients. And it had been a time in which I gradually learned to bring more of myself to our interactions. But I had a long commute to Cal State Long

Beach, and the work became increasingly demanding. I did like my job, but found I missed the one-on-one contact with patients.

Sitting at my desk one afternoon my mind wandered for a few minutes from the job I had to thoughts of chaplaincy as a profession. I picked up the phone and called the Reverend Janet Humphreys, who was Director of the Chaplain Services and the Clinical Pastoral Education (CPE) at UCLA. She was a fellow Presbyterian and we were acquainted. I asked her what my chances were for employment as a chaplain if I were to take the one-year training. Knowing I was not a clergyperson she told me, "Frankly, Pat, your chances are zero. Programs always want ordained clergy." I put that idea out of my mind. Perhaps there were other ways I could help and could nudge the church toward involvement.

During this time, I was shocked when my supervisor, Gary Humfleet, left his position. The transition was eased, however, when they hired Michael Prelip to fill the position. Mike had his Master's degree in public health. He was delightful to work with and taught me how to set up goals, objectives, and methods for our cooperative trainings.

In the break room there were big binders holding summaries of NIMH-funded studies. I liked reading them while I ate my lunch. There was one study on the role of churches in influencing attitudes toward people with HIV/AIDS. Teaching that AIDS was God's way of punishing homosexuals was clearly negative from a public health point of view, but of even greater interest to me was one on the problem of silence. If the pastor didn't speak about AIDS, then the parishioners tended to not speak about it, whether with the pastor or anyone else. In too many churches silence was the predominating reality with regard to AIDS. I started thinking about something I could develop to address the problem of silence.

I started phoning national denominational headquarters and asking about any work they were doing related to AIDS. When I phoned the United Methodists in New York, I was directed to a woman named Cathie Lyons with the Board of Global Ministries. I felt like we were friends from the beginning. Cathie was hard at work developing resources for local churches to encourage support of people in congregations who were dealing with AIDS. Over the phone, sight unseen, Cathie asked, "Would you write a resource for us on AIDS ministry?" "Yes, I'd be interested." This wouldn't be writing for my workplace, but on my own time.

The idea we came up with was to anchor the resource in stories from church-related people, mostly United Methodists, who had been touched by AIDS. Cathie supplied me with some contacts to add to those I already had. In my free time I began doing interviews, some in person and some by phone. The most memorable one (because it was personal to me) was an interview with Reverend Jim White, my friend in campus ministry at Cal State Long Beach. Soon after I had started the job he had invited me to take a walk around campus, acquainting me with its features. His most important agenda, however, was letting me get more deeply acquainted with him. He revealed to me that he was gay and had been diagnosed with HIV. When I started work on the Methodist resource, I asked Jim if I could interview him and include his story. He agreed but said his name and other identifiers could not be used. He was fearful about losing his job, a common problem at that time.

We ended up doing the taped interview on our lunch hour, folded into his little VW bug in the parking lot. Jim, sitting in the driver's seat, told me through tears how he had met with the pastor of the local church where he had taught adult education programs. He shared with the pastor that he had been diagnosed as HIV-positive. Jim had been hoping for comfort and support. Instead he experienced rejection. A few days after the meeting he received a letter from the church ending his teaching relationship with them and reducing their financial support of his ministry at the university by 90 percent.

This moving interview was another transition point in my inner and outer journey into AIDS ministry. He emphasized that the church's homophobia was an obstacle for ministry. Jim was trusting his story to me, and he was telling me there was an assignment out there in the institutional church to make a difference for gay people.

A few years later, I attended Jim's memorial service held at the United Church of Christ in Long Beach. (This was a gay-affirming congregation.) He had spent his many years as a clergyman in campus ministry and the service he planned reflected that world, including a procession of about twenty clergy wearing their robes, stoles, and hoods like at an academic baccalaureate, complete with a farewell sermon.

Cathie Lyons told me she was planning to be in California that June for the VI International AIDS Conference in San Francisco, and suggested we could meet if I attended.

I approached our director about allowing me my paid hours to attend the conference. He agreed if I could cover my own expenses and could identify four to six of the most relevant new developments which might suggest topics for the Physician Education Program.

I had written articles for *Christianity & Crisis*, an independent, progressive monthly magazine. I contacted Leon Howell, the editor, offering to write one or more articles on the AIDS Conference if he would supply me with a press pass, which would give me access to Conference events. He agreed to it. I let Cathie Lyons know it was a go for me to attend the conference, but I was still looking for free lodging. She gave me the names of a United Methodist clergy couple in the city and I contacted them. They graciously agreed to have me stay at their walk-up flat west of the Convention Center and near the light-rail line.

I arrived a couple of hours before the opening plenary session the day the convention began and found the press area, where I got my press badge. I had never had a press badge before and that would have been enough excitement for me. The opening plenary, however, became unforgettable. I was sitting alone far back in this huge auditorium, which was filling up with people from all around the world, though I suppose they were predominantly from the US. I don't remember if it was night or just seemed like night in the darkened auditorium, with the lighting primarily on the stage. There were several speakers and then a man was at the microphone and asked how many present were AIDS activists and would they please raise their hands. Looking out into the semi-darkened auditorium, few hands went up. I guess most attendees were scientists, doctors, or academics. I felt uncomfortable. Surely more than this dozen or two felt themselves morally bound to be activists in the midst of this terrible epidemic. Then the activists, few as there seemed to be, were asked to walk forward and come up on the stage. Without a single thought about my journalistic responsibilities to an unbiased view, and with my heart pounding, I stood up and made my way alone down the long aisle and up the stairs onto the stage, where I joined a small group of self-identified AIDS activists. A few minutes later I learned that this was a planned event by ACT UP. They must have been surprised to see this fiftyish woman they didn't know up there on stage with them. (ACT UP, or AIDS Coalition to Unleash Power, was a direct action advocacy group formed in 1987 in New York City under the leadership of Larry Kramer. They were trying, among other efforts, to speed up trials of new AIDS medications. They were known for their bold militancy.)

When I wasn't in sessions learning about new therapies, I would hang out in the bright, airy exhibit hall with friends I'd made in the Southern California Interfaith AIDS Coalition. The organization had an exhibit that was manned primarily by gay members who were happy to be in San Francisco. On one day, around lunch time, one of them announced he was going out to get his nipple pierced. I don't believe I was the only person who didn't want to think too much about that experience. He went out, had the piercing done and returned in a surprisingly short time. There in the brightness of the exhibit hall he excitedly unbuttoned his shirt to show us the new sexy hardware. No one seemed the least bit uncomfortable including me in their circle. I loved that and remember it today with a smile.

Cathie Lyons and I met on the street during the joyous San Francisco Gay Pride Parade. Meeting in person added warmth and humanity to our work together on what would come to be called *AIDS Ministry: A Practical Guide for Pastors,* a resource to help pastors and laity bring AIDS out of the closet and into the sanctuaries, offices, and conversations of the church, and to do so with the sensitivity and kindness the people I interviewed were asking for.

I would stay in touch with Cathie as I continued doing interviews and preparing a resource section for the book. Sometime in this process I was saddened to learn that Cathie had been let go. I never knew the details. My project was continued under her replacement, Charles Carnahan.

In the fall of 1990, the county interagency training team that we participated in decided to offer a training in "Spiritual Issues in Mental Health Services when HIV-infected Clients are Served." I think I originated the idea, but it may have emerged among three of us: myself, Bryan Mershon, PhD, who was in charge of HIV/AIDS services for Los Angeles County's Department of Mental Health, and Rosa Kaplan, DSW. In any case, the three of us from the training team put together a training in spiritual perspectives directed at mental health professionals, and which was eligible for continuing education credits. My husband, Cecil, a clinical psychologist and a clergyman, agreed to lead a segment. I put together the materials. It was a chance for me to practice what I had been learning and apply it in an area close to my heart, offering spiritual support in the AIDS-affected community.

On December 3, 1990, sixteen motivated mental health professionals, mostly clinical social workers, attended the half-day program. They let us know how much they needed and wanted training in how to support their

HIV clients and in how to avoid burn-out themselves. Recalling this event, I especially remember Bryan, who had been raised in a very conservative religious environment. Together we had a chance to bring more life-giving spiritual perspectives than he had experienced before.

Looking back at that December program, which was different from all the other trainings we had presented in Los Angeles County, I realize the inner voice calling me to spiritually support people with HIV/AIDS was still speaking.

Cecil and I made a decision, which had long been generating, to leave the Los Angeles area and move to Ventura, California, about sixty miles up the coast. Cecil was leaving his position with a mental health clinic he had founded. He would be starting a private practice in Ventura. Knowing that would take some time, I was especially motivated to find work up that way so I could contribute financially.

As spring approached and our May departure came into view, Mike Prelip did all he could to provide me with leads for AIDS-related work in Ventura County, but the prospects were not good. The county had a much smaller population and a much smaller HIV/AIDS population, and therefore fewer jobs in that field. The positions in existence were mostly in health services, positions for nurses and social workers. It didn't look as if an unusual opportunity like I enjoyed at Cal State Long Beach would be available anytime soon. The experience, however, of working with this largely gay, professional staff to make a difference in how people with HIV/AIDS were treated, would stay with me.

On May 30, 1991, we made our move to Ventura. Moving to Ventura meant living closer to two of our three children, which was a big plus for us. One of our daughters, Mary, had been living in Ventura for several years. Our other daughter, Ruth, and her husband were living just north in Santa Barbara. (Our son Bruce and his family were living northeast of Los Angeles in Hesperia. He would later move to Ventura, too.) On June 1st, we drove to Santa Barbara to celebrate Ruth's 29th birthday at a party in a park. I had to hold onto these positive experiences because so much about the first year was challenging.

Through the summer I applied for several jobs I didn't get. None were related to AIDS, but my desire to work in that field had not died. I was getting to know people and networking.

In mid-September, I accepted a hectic, eight-week job trying belatedly to pull together a man's campaign for city council. Our house filled up with campaign literature. Campaign volunteers were working in our family room. I was accompanying our candidate to events.

There were positive features in this mad job (in addition to being paid). I learned a lot about Ventura's streets and neighborhoods, its major businesses, its philanthropists, and got acquainted with its leading progressives. On November 5th, our candidate lost, but at least I knew where I was.

6

The Call Becomes Clarified

Recession, the very factor that made it hard for me to find a job in Ventura in 1991-92 became my ticket to work. I dragged out my grant writing training from the seventies and set up a consulting practice for nonprofits which were struggling to attract funding in a bad economy and couldn't afford to hire staff to write funding proposals. I did work for half a dozen nonprofits, including the City of Ventura's Department of Parks and Recreation. I ended up working part-time for Turning Point, an independent mental health agency serving the poor. I loved the projects these groups were working on and was glad to help them seek funding, but the work didn't make my heart sing.

One day, while sitting at my writing desk at home reading the mail, I saw an item in the Presbyterian newsletter specifically stating that UCLA's Clinical Pastoral Education (CPE) program accepted laity. This was the very program whose director I had contacted two years earlier, and who frankly told me that, as a layperson, I had zero chance of being hired as a chaplain. I knew her warning was rational and intended to spare me disappointment, but I suddenly knew I needed to pursue this, all evidence to the contrary.

For me the article was a message from the sacred sphere. That very day I phoned and asked how to apply. My completed application was in the mail within a week and I was set up for an appointment. I drove in to UCLA for my interview with the Reverend Dave Jenkins. He accepted me for a half-time unit beginning September 14, 1992. The full program for preparing for chaplaincy is four units which can be completed in one year. By going half-time, I would be able to complete only one unit in six months, but considering it was one hundred twenty miles round-trip and I would be continuing my consulting business, half-time made sense.

Orientation to the UCLA Medical Center was on a Tuesday. We learned the location of the Emergency Room, which is a regional Trauma Center, and got acquainted with the various floors, some with their own ICUs. It wasn't until the following Sunday that this information took on critical meaning. Late in the week I learned that I would be the on-call chaplain that Sunday from 5 p.m. until the next morning! I thought they were out of their minds entrusting this responsibility to a laywoman with two days of training. Many taking CPE have finished theological seminary and were taking one required unit of CPE. I figured they might be better prepared. Or they should leave on-call to the more advanced people, those in their second, third, or fourth units.

At 5 p.m. Sunday evening, I was handed the on-call pager by a more experienced CPE student who was going off duty. I was too flummoxed to inquire how the thing worked. After he left, I studied it trying to figure it out. I spent most of the evening alone in the office, glancing compulsively at the pager to see if it did anything unusual that might signal that I was being paged. It stayed in stasis and continued that way through a restless night in a vacant hospital room assigned as the Chaplain's Sleep Room. By the grace of God I was not called to minister to any patient that first Sunday night. Monday morning, with a full day of training ahead, I did ask for instruction in using the pager.

The first week I and my CPE cohort got set up with our pastoral care assignments. I was assigned the Medical/Surgical unit, seeing patients following a wide variety of surgeries. But my supervisor, Dave Jenkins, gave me permission to explore doing some of my pastoral care hours near home at Ventura County Medical Center's (VCMC) weekly Immunology Clinic, which served HIV/AIDS patients. That medical center had no history of having chaplains.

I wrote to Dr. John Prichard, the Medical Director of the Immunology Clinic, and proposed serving there as an unpaid chaplain intern. He promptly called me in for an interview with him and agreed to try me out. This was an exciting opportunity, my first chance to be in AIDS Ministry. However, since outpatient chaplaincy was on the cutting edge, there were few guidelines for how to go about it.

I started at the clinic Tuesday, September 22, 1992, with the weekly 7:30 a.m. case conference. There were about eight staff, including nurses, social workers, a psychologist, Dr. Prichard, and sometimes other county staff who would join us. At fifty-seven, I was the oldest person, and I had this religious title, Chaplain. These were reasons for some to treat me coolly. I felt they wondered what I had to contribute that they would value. Perhaps it was me wondering what I had to contribute. Their tasks were so well defined: address the patients' health problems; help patients with their needs for food or housing; and assist them with signing up for public assistance, Medicaid, or special AIDS programs. But what was I offering?

Early in October, after case conference, Dr. Prichard asked me to make a home patient visit to Dave. I was pleased he was asking me to do this. It felt like an affirmation. I was so caught up in the experience of having the medical director give me an assignment that it didn't occur to me to ask why specifically he wanted me to go. He did say something about home visits being a part of family practice medicine, his specialty, and that he himself made home visits.

Dave, who was about thirty, was back living with his parents because he was no longer well enough to work. On the day of my visit, his parents weren't home. Lacking clear goals and too new to know the distinctive tasks of a chaplain, I simply used the time to get acquainted with Dave. The visit was not memorable apart from being my first home visit, but the story he shared, placing him in relationship to his mother and father, would prove valuable a few months later.

The CPE training was exciting and demanding. I was at UCLA Medical Center two days a week for training and for my chaplaincy assignment at the hospital in the Medical/Surgical unit. Then, every other Sunday evening, I drove back to UCLAMC for my turn at being on-call, spent the night, and was on deck Monday morning for the new week of training. Tuesdays were in Ventura at VCMC's Immunology Clinic.

The setting for my Tuesday morning ministry was challenging. At that time, the Immunology Clinic was housed in a large mobile unit, set up with offices at one end, along with the conference room we crowded into to hear cases, and examining rooms at the other end. In between was a large waiting area where patients entered the mobile unit and found a chair along the wall on one side or the other. This waiting room was the main place where I worked. Typically there would be maybe a dozen men and women in the room. (For the first time I was meeting women with HIV, though they were a small percentage of our patients.)

I would sit down next to a patient and introduce myself. They some-times asked what a chaplain was, which gave me the opportunity to keep thinking about what I was there for. To love them? To want to hear their stories? To convey empathy? To be the face of institutional religion without condemnation and without dogmas? Some patients were relaxed and open with me. Others were standoffish for months. I couldn't blame them.

After about a month of case conferences and talking with patients in the waiting room, I was beginning to get a sense of the population we were serving. One day I asked Craig Webb, a social worker on the team, what percentage of the patients had drug or alcohol addictions. He said more than 90 percent were either in recovery or still struggling with substance abuse.

I didn't operate with a wariness about our patients with addictions. One of them, a guy in recovery, noticed where I left my purse each week. "You know, Pat, you should put your purse out of sight," he told me. On his advice I did from then on.

Ventura County had a drug and alcohol addiction program. One of their staff, Sam Gill, came to the Immunology Clinic on Tuesdays to check in with patients who were clients of his. He facilitated a large twelve-step group for people with HIV/AIDS. One day I asked him how I could get more educated about addictions and what our patients were facing. He gave me some literature to read. Then he invited me to sit in with his group. He probably checked in with his group to see how they felt about having me at-tend. Then he invited me to co-facilitate four meetings in which I led them in a spiritual support segment using a *lectio divina* process. On retreat the year before I had learned a group method of doing *lectio divina,* an ancient way of praying with short passages of Scripture or other reflective texts. In this method, one is listening for the voice of the sacred, unmediated by any religious authority. I thought at the time that it would be a good group practice with gay men and others in the HIV/AIDS community.

Leading and listening in this twelve-step group was a privilege and a significant learning opportunity for me. Out of this experience, any illusory wall of separation I had felt between myself and clinic patients I knew to have drug addictions dissolved. Demolishing that wall in my mind opened the way for deeper contact with patients in great need and great pain.

At the clinic, one of the standoffish patients was "Hank," a big, good look-ing heterosexual guy who had contracted HIV doing injectable drugs. By the time I knew him he was a committed twelve-stepper who had served as a sponsor for many others. He had been a Roman Catholic but had left the church. He was courteous to me, but didn't want any involvement with whatever it was I was doing. I did get to know his wife "Catherine" when she accompanied Hank as his health deteriorated and his visits to the clinic became more frequent.

One Tuesday, I learned in case conference that Hank was very ill and in the hospital. During the morning, Catherine came looking for me. Hank wanted me to hear his confession. I suggested I could call a priest, but she said he didn't want a priest. He wanted me.

I hurried over to his room on the hospital's third floor. He was conscious but unable to communicate clearly. We did establish that he had asked for me and I was there to hear his confession. It was difficult to understand what he was sharing. But after each remembered burden, when he would pause I would simply say, "God offers you forgiveness." This went on for maybe twenty minutes and when he was finished I said my goodbyes, the last I would ever say to him. I returned to clinic feeling utterly worn out by the strain to listen, the awareness of what it meant that he had called for me, the confidence he was placing in me, and the almost certain knowledge that I would not see him again. He died a day or two later.

During that first unit of CPE, my supervisor, Dave Jenkins, made the sixty-mile drive out to Ventura to see the clinic in operation and to meet with Dr. Prichard. He was extremely empathetic to the difficulties the whole situation presented to this chaplain-in-training. I appreciated having Dave see and validate the challenges of doing outpatient chaplaincy in a setting with little or no privacy, with young men and women suddenly facing death, many with few coping skills.

7

Developing in Ministry

In order to have more time and to engage in greater depth with some patients I was connecting with, I decided to offer a small group during December calling it Spiritual Questing. It would use the *lectio divina* process I had tried in the twelve-step group. Dr. Prichard gave his approval for the group, so I made up fliers on lilac paper (which became my signature paper), making them available at the clinic during November. I also got the word out to the Countywide AIDS Task Force and to PFLAG (Parents and Friends of Lesbians and Gays). This was a new venture for me and a new idea for our patients. Out of about 150 patients, nine responded and four actually showed up for the evening group held once a week during December. I used only the group *lectio divina* process as I had learned it from its originator, Norvene Vest (though it goes back hundreds of years as an individual contemplative practice.). I utilized Norvene's book, *Bible Reading for Spiritual Growth*, in my preparation.

I rented a small room at the Church of Religious Science in downtown Ventura. The four men came faithfully each week and entered into the meditative process with a good spirit. At the end of the final session, when I asked for feedback, they all said they liked it and hoped I would offer it again. One participant, Sam, who came quite a distance, from Thousand Oaks, said the meetings were too short and maybe I could add something if I did it again.

It would be two years before I would have a chance to offer it a second time, but I kept their evaluations in mind and used them when the new opportunity came along.

Dr. Prichard took me aside one Tuesday to say that Dave, the man with whom I did my first home visit, had been brought into the ER by his parents. He wanted me to go see him. The VCMC ER was only a few yards across the way from the Immunology Clinic, but it was totally unknown territory for me. When I went in I was directed to a quiet area. There was Dave's mother, whom I had gotten to know when she would drive Dave to the clinic. She was sitting alone in a waiting area. I learned that Dave was on an examining table (or was it a bed?), in a large room with subdued lighting, alone. I went in and spoke with him, and asked if there was anything I could do for him. He said he wanted to speak with each of his parents and asked if I would bring them to him.

Without being told, I knew he was dying. My brain was taking it in without consciously processing it. I knew ERs are busy places, running on the adrenaline of doctors and nurses working to save people's lives. No one was in this room with Dave at the time. I knew without thinking about it that meant they had nothing more to offer him than the chance for quiet.

Sensing the urgency of his situation, how little time he might have left, I hurried out to his mother and asked where her husband was. She didn't know. He had gotten up to move around. When I found him, I told him Dave wanted to speak with him and asked him to please come right away. I brought him into the room and then left them alone while I went out to sit with Dave's mother. A little later, Dave's father came out and his mother went in. I left to return to the clinic. Within two or three hours Dave slipped into a coma and that night he died.

A month later, Dave's mother came to the Tuesday clinic to thank the staff for their care of her son. She spoke to me separately, sharing a story about that last day in the ER. Dave and his dad, she explained, had had a hard time getting along. But on the last day of his life Dave bridged over that alienation. He thanked his dad for all the times he had fixed his cars over the years. This meant so much to Dave's father. It was a thrill to me that I had helped facilitate the delivery of that gift.

Jimmy's family were devoted Baptists, as was Jimmy. I think AIDS had outed him at church. The pastor started pointedly speaking about his "sin" in Sunday morning sermons. Jimmy had enough compassion for himself to stop attending. I got to know him at the clinic, and as he became sicker and his mother brought him, she and I would talk. They were both caring, warm people.

I went to see Jimmy in the ICU when he was near the end of his life. He was very weak, but acknowledged me. I prayed with him and then, when I started to leave, he beckoned me back with his red-lit index finger with the blood oxygen monitor clipped on it. He took my hand.

His nurse, Don, came in bringing one of Jimmy's favorite CDs, one by Barbara Streisand. The first track was "Somewhere" from *West Side Story*. Tears welled up in my eyes as I listened to the song and thought about what it would have meant to Jimmy to live long enough to experience a place in our society for his love. He smiled, listening to the words. I stayed by the bed with him holding my hand for an hour and a half. He slept lightly most of that time. He died four days later. In the years since, hearing that recording always makes me think of Jimmy and always makes me cry. Dear Jimmy, if only you could have lived to see the changes.

I had met Tim before I ever started at the clinic. He was a quiet but assertive voice for acceptance, assistance, and justice for people living with AIDS in our county. He was an independent man, an artist, who had reached deep for spiritual resources to live with AIDS. From time to time, both before and after I became the chaplain at the clinic, Tim would contact me if he needed help. Tim, like many AIDS patients I have known, didn't want to be treated like a victim in need of sympathy. His invitations suggested that he experienced me as appreciating how he was living his life.

I remember Tim taking me through his apartment, showing me his paintings, his innovative art furniture, his fish ponds and herb garden, and my thinking about the courage and determination it took for him to continue living at such a level with advanced AIDS. I also thought about what a loss we were soon going to experience. I often was mute in the presence of his life and his personal spirituality.

My last visit with Tim was in the hospital. The unit was short-staffed and Tim had some needs he asked me to assist with. I had gotten his bedding more comfortable and had helped him turn on his side for the night. Having turned him I stroked his back. He enjoyed it and asked me to continue. When it was enough he told me, "Now scratch the hell out of it," which I did. Throughout this time he was free-associating about lovers he had known, a photograph taken of him at the beach with a bow in his hair, the comfort of backrubs from a lover. His mind was taking a vacation from pain and illness.

Tim died of AIDS at age thirty-five. We all missed him.

With Tim I learned something of the place of silence, reception, and the sacramental quality of the ordinary when God seems present.

Adding to the emotional challenges for me during this period was my mother's declining health. My mother was living in Palm Springs. Her well-thought-out arrangements were excellent in most respects. Her first-floor apartment was on Tahquitz Canyon Road with a very nice mall and her bank across the street and bus service at the corner. She had friends nearby, but none of our family lived close. She had had several small strokes and transient ischemic attacks (TIAs), some of which were accompanied by falls. It was hard for me to get good information because my mother had as little to do with doctors as possible. One day, our daughter Ruth called me to say she had just been speaking with my mother and something was not right. My mother had told her she had been sitting at the desk writing but she couldn't recall why. Then she had turned on the TV, but couldn't manage to change the stations. I phoned Mother and heard the sort of slurred speech that is typical of strokes. I told her to stay seated on her sofa and that I would call Sharon, her hairdresser and friend who lived nearby, and ask her to come. Sharon was home and went right over. She called and notified me she was taking Mother to the ER.

I let Cecil know I needed to drive out to Palm Springs, packed a bag, and set out for the hospital where Mother had been admitted for observation. She would be released the next day. I took her to the doctor for her follow-up appointment and finally got clear information. She had narrowing of the arteries and needed to be on medication.

The trips out to the desert had become frequent. Sharon let me know that Mother was asking more and more of her and she wanted to help but had her own family to take care of. I encouraged Mother to think about letting us help her move to an apartment in Ventura. The next day, as I prepared to drive the four hours home, I felt spent. How was I going to do this along with CPE? As I drove west and north out of Palm Springs it had been raining lightly. When I got to the on-ramp for Interstate 10, there was a huge rainbow before me. It looked like I would drive right through it, but instead it seemed to move just ahead of me for miles, like a sign from heaven encouraging me. A few months later, the whole family showed up to help my mother move to an apartment near us in Ventura.

The final evaluation process for my first unit of CPE involved the four of us who were being supervised by Dave meeting together as he gave us feedback. Part of his feedback was telling me that when he first interviewed me he didn't think I'd make it through the unit. He thought I would be too fragile. I don't know what he picked up on, but I know that it is easier for me to function if I'm clear that I've been given the authority for a task. The CPE program offered me authority to minister to people. The relationship with my supervisor emboldened me to let myself be visible and active without fear of retribution.

One Tuesday at the Immunology Clinic, Doug Green showed up. He was the new director of AIDS Care, a small, secular, social service agency. AIDS Care served some of the clinic clients with a food distribution program and other services. Doug seemed to be at the clinic that day mainly to meet clinic staff. I realize now that hiring Doug had been a coup for this little nonprofit, which had been a three-person staff originally, but under Doug, was expanding. We found a somewhat private spot at one end of the waiting room to get acquainted. Doug had an MBA and had been in banking. He had taken an extended amount of time off for self-exploration and to decide what he wanted to do with the rest of his life. When the AIDS Care position opened up, he responded. He told me about his family, which was Presbyterian, and that as a kid he had liked their pastor. He was pleased to learn that I was a Presbyterian, even though he himself had left the church over the gay issue and had become a Buddhist. There was an easy rapport between us. We would continue developing our friendship on clinic days over the next months.

8

Claiming an Incarnational Ministry

Eight months passed before I started a second extended unit of CPE. For me, the eight-month interim period was full. I continued as a chaplain intern at the Immunology Clinic. We settled Mother in a small apartment near us in Ventura (a major adjustment for us both). The United Methodist resource I had written was finally published by the Board of Global Ministries with the title *HIV/AIDS Ministry, a Practical Guide for Pastors.* In addition, I was continuing to write funding proposals for nonprofits.

The Reverend Dave Jenkins, my first CPE supervisor, left to take a position at a hospital in Houston. When I started my second extended CPE unit in December 1993, the Reverend Karen Schnell was my new supervisor. The second unit continued the pattern of Mondays and Thursdays at UCLAMC for training and chaplaincy experience, this time in the large Neonatal ICU, with Tuesdays in Ventura at the Immunology Clinic. And, as before, I was on-call at UCLA every other weekend. Being entrusted to minister as a chaplain at this major medical center was in the column of encouragements. Other people expecting I could do this seemed to be the key to unlock my abilities.

I had several memorable ministry experiences during this unit. They were opportunities for me to grow, and to fall in love with chaplaincy. One of them was at the very beginning of my second CPE unit. I had been assigned to UCLA Medical Center's large and very busy Neonatal ICU (NICU).

The first day, I walked in to introduce myself and found the staff— about twelve doctors and nurses—huddled around an examining table. I knew there must be a code, some infant in mortal danger. Christine, the social worker, saw me, "Oh, I'm so glad you came. I just called down to

Pastoral Care and got the answering machine. We have a baby they are trying to revive. The mother is in the hospital. She's a single mom and is here alone. We have an overhead page for her. I'm afraid the baby will die before she gets up here. She speaks only Spanish and has a speech impediment." All the time she was speaking she was moving around, glancing through the little window in the door of the neonatal unit, looking down the long hallway.

Everything was rushed. There was so much that needed to be done. I was trying to get my bearings, trying to find out what I needed to know. Then the mother, Juana— heavy young woman who had been living at the hospital for days— was there. Christine told her in Spanish that the baby was in trouble. Tears and shock followed. I was introduced to her as we moved into a conference room.

She was crying and speaking. I couldn't understand her words, just held her, kissed her, smelled the oiliness of her unwashed hair, stroked her, and tried to be her mother.

Christine moved in and out of the room, getting information and bringing it back, bringing in a nurse and Ishmael, a young maintenance man who spoke Spanish, then the doctor, a Spanish speaker. The doctor talked too fast and said too much. I knew Juana wasn't taking it in. He probably didn't want this duty, and was himself in distress. He said, "We're doing all we can" and then listed the procedures. Juana didn't care about that. She knew her baby was dying. Her only one, her *lindo*, her Juan, named for her I expect.

They all left. I saw her Spanish Bible there on the table before her. It was worn. On the flyleaf were names scrawled by other people who had had that Bible before she did, like in a school textbook. Her name, Juana, was halfway down the page in large, round cursive letters. There were a lot of bookmarkers in her Bible. One marker was at Psalm 23. I asked in my elemental Spanish if this was a favorite passage. She nodded yes. Would she like me to read it? Yes, again. I read slowly trying to pronounce the words with as much accuracy as I could. About halfway through I felt it was too challenging and stopped.

I asked what church she attended and who was her pastor. She had all her numbers organized in a small, personal phone book with no cover. She turned to her pastor's number and on a slip of paper she had, she wrote his name and number. I asked for the name of the church. Church was held in the pastor's home. She was an evangelical, a poor woman who carried the name and number of her pastor with her.

Christine returned. She took this new information and tried to reach the pastor, as she had tried to contact sisters. Some were coming, but the pastor was not answering.

The Spanish-speaking doctor, a clinical nurse specialist, and a couple of other people returned. Juan had died.

I thought about where to put myself. I had stood up and lost my seat next to Juana. I stood by her, holding her. She was distraught. The doctor was speaking more slowly this time, sitting opposite her, watching her as he spoke. They tried everything he told her. The baby had many problems. Even if his heart had not failed, he might not have been able to survive long with all those problems. He wanted her to understand that it was better for the infant to die. The baby had spent all of his three or four months of life in hospitals. The doctor stopped speaking and looked at Juana, who was weeping. Compassion filled his face, and he asked if she had any questions. Her only question was the one she kept asking later, when they moved her into a little private room and brought her baby, her *lindo. Porque, El Senor? Porque mi lindo?*

Sitting beside her on the small couch in the tiny, private room, I had my arm around her and she was holding her little baby. So pretty, such delicate, well-defined features. Almost all of his black hair had been shaved away and tiny red spots marked the places where IVs had been placed. I touched the little bare head; he was still warm. She was crying and speaking to the baby and to God. My first tears came, but I brought them under control in less than a minute.

Christine entered with a tall Hispanic man. Mr. Meza happened onto the unit to get a phone number. He was a member of the parents' support group. He sat on the chair, knee-to-knee with Juana. He was wonderful, soothing, sympathetic.

After a while I was thinking, "She needs to hand over this dead baby." I didn't know if it had been long enough or too long. I didn't know. I suggested we have prayer and Mr. Meza could translate. I said everything I wanted to say to the woman. I spoke of what a good mother she had been, how she had given everything she had to give, all her love and attention, to this baby. I asked that God would receive this baby into his loving hands (Juana would no doubt think of God as male), and I asked that God would comfort this good woman and gradually help her to find new life after this great loss. Then I silently indicated to Mr. Meza that it might be time to take the baby. He took the little form himself, so tenderly, then sat a minute or two, talking with Juana. Then he left with the dead baby.

A few minutes later, Juana and Christina were going into the NICU. They came back out and reentered the tiny private room. The sign on the door said it was a room for nursing babies. Christina told me that the mother wanted more time with the baby. A nurse once again wheeled the little body in in its rolling, plastic bassinette. She handed the little form in its white receiving blanket to the mother and covered it with an additional receiving blanket, as though it were alive and might get a chill.

That time, the mother was sitting in the chair. Mr. Meza, Christine, and I were crowded in, sitting and standing. The mother was speaking softly to the baby. She was praying, though I could understand little of it. Then she stopped and handed the baby to Mr. Meza to take away. He told me she had given the baby to God. She did this in her own time because she needed to pray. She needed to give him up. I'm proud of her, proud that she could assert herself to do what she needed to do. And maybe I helped her a little to know what she needed to do.

She thanked me and gave me a kiss. We found a phone and she called her pastor. He was home. They had a long talk and then she said he would be coming. After two hours, I said goodbye, walking off the unit into the empty hallway softly expelling, "my God, my God," and wanting to see a friend.

Another meaningful encounter with a clinic patient in Ventura was with Sam, one of the men who came to that first Spiritual Questing group. Sam was coming into the clinic often during 1992 and 1993. In February of 1993, he was hospitalized with PCP and another kind of pneumonia. I went to visit him. I had recently attended an all-day workshop on prayer traditions, including breath prayers. This is a practice of repeating a short prayer, calling on the sacred during the in-breath and repeating a brief petition with the exhalation. Before making this visit, I wrote some breath prayers for Sam. When I saw him I shared my newly learned information on breath prayers and said that I had written some for him. Would he like me to leave them for him to use? Pointing to the oxygen machine that he was hooked up to next to the bed, he said, with his usual humor, "Pat, I have two kinds of pneumonia. Rather than breath prayers, do you have any affirmations?" Oh, good alternative for someone struggling to breathe. I came up with some affirmations that we used as prayers with silence after each one. Sam told me the prayer "felt good."

Karen Schnell, my new supervisor, met with each of us individually and went over our reports on patient visits and discussed how things were going. I was older than most of the other interns, and less overtly religious. I also tended to see things more psychologically than spiritually. (And frankly have never seen a great separation between them.) For some supervisors this would have been a challenge, but she helped me claim myself as a chaplain. In one of our one-on-one meetings, she put a word to my style of ministry: incarnational. I had a passion for valuing each patient I met, listening for each story, and searching to understand who this person was. It was a way of ministering that I imagined Jesus engaged in. I think we are passionate to offer that which we most missed growing up.

I still have the box I decorated as an art project for my evaluation of the second unit at UCLAMC. It was one of those specialty boxes you don't want to discard. The theme of what I put on its several surfaces was "opening." (Opening the box, of course, was perfect for the theme.) Under the lid I wrote "Opening up to God wherever God is present" and included a B.C. cartoon showing the primitive man on his knees in the desert asking, "God, if you're up there give me a sign." In the next frame a marquee-size sign drops to the ground in front of B.C. The sign reads, "I'm up here!" Below the cartoon I wrote, and "in there, in them, down here, around there." On the inside bottom surface I wrote, "and opening up to my gifts and limits" and I listed the gifts as "hearing, writing, speaking, organizing, advocating, caring, and laughing," and included a favorite psychiatrist cartoon by Suzy Becker. (I never miss a day of reading the comics.) On one flap I pasted a quote from Carl Rogers, the psychologist who helped found person-centered psychotherapy, "What I am is good enough, if only I can be it openly. When I am up against a difficult situation, what I am inside is good enough to meet that situation if only I can be it openly."[1] Rogers's insight spoke to me. I had hidden my strengths and abilities from my parents, fearing their negative reaction if I seemed able to have an independent life. Later, the fear was maintained in a society which generally did not reward women who showed too much independence. Times had changed and I was trying to change my own brain, my thinking pattern. On the final surface I wrote, "I

1. Rogers, *On Becoming a Person*, 51.

have heard a call and I'm learning my curriculum about losses, death, and peace." I included a graphic from Church World News with the figure of a person with a heart and the quote from Isaiah 61, "Yahweh has sent me to bring good news to the poor, to bind up hearts that are broken, to proclaim liberty to captives." That was my call.

As the unit drew to a close in late spring of 1994, it was clear that finishing four units at UCLAMC was going to be too much. The long commute two or three times a week for another year was not sustainable.

9

New Opportunities

There was a small CPE program at a nearby Catholic hospital: St. John's in Oxnard. I applied there and was accepted as a full-time intern to begin a third CPE unit in September 1994. A disappointment to me was that they could not release me to continue pastoral care work at the Immunology Clinic. The program was small and they needed all their CPE interns to do spiritual care at this busy hospital. When I started at St. John's I chose to work on their large maternity/gynecology unit and their small neonatal ICU. Knowing I was disappointed to not be able to continue my AIDS ministry, they asked if I would like to take over facilitation of a weekly family support group offered at the hospital for family members of people with HIV/AIDS, for which they would pay me. The group was being facilitated by Pickens Halt, a marriage and family therapist on the hospital staff. She was moving toward retirement and wanted to give up this evening responsibility.

What an opportunity! One benefit was it put me close with family members of people with HIV/AIDS. Pickens was willing to help me get acquainted with the group, and in the longer term, she became my mentor in doing grief work.

Pickens had a specialty in grief counseling and her mentoring was not only helpful for the family support group, but in my ministry with the hospital's young parents whose babies died at or near birth. Pickens's office was just across from the NICU. I could check in with her when problems arose. Her mentoring on grief care was another benefit.

Getting to know the people associated with the support group was a blessing. Muriel Steiger had been an early member of the group. After her son died, she made herself available to facilitate when I needed to be away. She had training in small-group facilitation. Another person available to help facilitate, and an ongoing member of the group, was Terry Monk. Terry was about my age and a sixteen-year survivor of AIDS at the time I met him. He brought a wonderful presence to the meetings and wanted to be a support to these parents. It was a long time before I realized that Terry never told his own mother that he was infected. His older brother had died of AIDS and he didn't think she could stand knowing he had the disease too. Terry was a multitalented man. He had been a leading man in musical theater and was a wonderful trained group leader. He was a builder who could construct almost anything. He would phone me at home from time to time and when I'd answer he'd say, "It's the Monk." We were friends right up to his death some years later, which occurred not long after his mother's death. He never had to tell her of his diagnosis.

Sam, who had been in that first Spiritual Questing group, kept track of where I was. I got a call one day at St. John's from Sam's mother saying he would like to see me. He was very ill and in the ICU at VCMC. Each patient had a small, individual room with large windows. I never saw much equipment in these rooms in the several times I visited patients there who were near the end of their lives.

The evening I visited Sam, he was on a ventilator, a device that goes in the mouth and down the trachea, breathing for the patient. Because of the vent he couldn't talk, but he had paper and a pen. I asked if he had a particular reason for wanting me to come. (It seems I had learned to ask questions.) He responded by writing out some end-of-life requests, in a barely legible scrawl, including his wishes for cremation and scattering and for me to speak about him at a home funeral. I told him I would assist his family and friends to carry out his wishes. Before I left, I asked, "Would you like me to pray with you, Sam?" He nodded yes. How to pray with a nonreligious man facing his death? How to support his evident interest in attending to his spiritual life through the two years I had known him? The noisy ventilator, pumping air, keeping him alive, became my inspiration. My prayer for him was, that with every breath from the ventilator, he might experience God's Spirit present with him, that he would see he was never alone, and always filled with God.

The next day I phoned Sam's mother to ask if the family had discussed any arrangements for the time of Sam's death. She said they had not. I recommended selecting a mortuary and giving that mortuary some information about what Sam and the family would be wanting. I also encouraged her to talk with Sam about his wish to have his ashes scattered at sea.

A few days later I made my weekly trip to the Ventura Farmer's Market. In addition to the usual produce for Cecil and me, I bought a big bouquet of yellow spider chrysanthemums for Sam. I stopped by the hospital on my way home and took them up to his little room. Of course they weren't arranged, just a big bouquet of flowers with long stems. A nurse gave me a large Styrofoam cup to put them in.

Sam was better and off the ventilator, but he didn't want to speak much, because his throat was sore. I apologized for not having arranged the flowers, but I had just brought them from the market, I explained. He was sitting up in bed. He looked over at the flowers and then at me and made a gesture with both hands up and out, just like the flowers themselves. He had a sweet expression of gratitude.

Sam had survived another bout and was able to be home for Thanksgiving and Christmas, although he was very weak and required a home health aide.

In January, I got a call from his sister saying he had died and he had wanted me to do a memorial service for him. The family was religiously unaffiliated and seemed glad to have someone Sam had chosen to do the service. It was a simple service, some lighted candles, his brother sang, there were family recollections, and I spoke about Sam, as I had promised him I would. We included Psalm 23, as requested by his mother. We concluded with a prayer I had written for the occasion.

As a laywoman conducting the service, I thought about what I should wear. I don't remember what I settled on, but I do remember including a narrow, handwoven stole around my neck. The stole which clergy wear originated, as I understand it, with the towel, a sign of service to others. I had bought this stole, woven in Guatemala, to wear on sacramental occasions. Wearing it said, at least to me, I'm here to offer a sacred service. It was an outer sign that helped me incorporate my new identity as chaplain.

But just in case I might get too carried away with my new religious identity, let me tell you what happened after the service. During the reception, Sam's sister told me he had often spoken about me, always referring to me as "the church lady." That was a surprise. I believe he was a little embarrassed for his family to know how close he was with this chaplain. So, he needed to refer to me as "the church lady," famous to anyone who watched *Saturday Night Live*. I was not offended.

Four years earlier, I had been sitting in another living room for another home memorial, painfully witnessing the absence of any support from the church. The church was like a storehouse of spiritual support which was locked away from a suffering community. I was only one, and a layperson at that. But now I was able to be here for this man, for this family, for the AIDS-affected community where I lived. I could bring some of what the church had—and has—to offer, and myself and my heart to say goodbye to Sam.

Full-time CPE was demanding. I could work fifty hours a week with the time it took to write up "verbatims," (word-for-word accounts of patient encounters that were used to critique our work) and engage in my on-call and pastoral care hours. I was often tired in the morning as I drove from home in Ventura the several miles to St. John's in Oxnard. On the way, I would prepare myself for the day by singing an ancient prayer from the Sarum Primer of 1514. I had learned it from a favorite recording by the Cambridge Trinity College Choir. Here are the words:

> *God be in my head and in my understanding;*
> *God be in mine eyes and in my looking;*
> *God be in my mouth and in my speaking;*
> *God be in my heart and in my thinking;*
> *God be at mine end, and at my departing.*[2]

I loved that this ancient prayer expressed a theology that matched my own, that God is in us, immanent, as well as all around us. Protestant churches in the US in the fifties, sixties, and seventies had overdosed on a different image of God as the all-powerful, all-knowing, triumphant, transcendent God. That felt a long way off to me, and uninvolved with my normal life. This prayer, as it prepared me for the day, reset my compass for where to look for God, and how to listen for God's word coming to me. God became more intimate, and also more omnipresent. This was underscored by my CPE training with my supervisor, Elizabeth Cook.

I got a phone call at home one day from Sandra DeGroot, an acquisitions editor with Eerdmans Publishing. An artist friend, John Swanson, had given her my book, *Ministry of the Dispossessed,* to read on a flight from Los

2

Angeles to Michigan. She wanted to know if I would write something for them. I told her I was in clinical pastoral education, doing fifty-hour weeks and couldn't think about a writing project at that time. But I added, "I have a manuscript in my files. It's a journal I kept for eighteen months when I was visiting AIDS patients in L. A. Would you want to see it?" She said she would and asked if I'd send a couple of chapters. I was thrilled at this opportunity. In fact, I was too excited to clarify about sending chapters. The journal wasn't divided into chapters. It was a day-by-day journal. I phoned my friend, Greg Dobie, who had read the manuscript a couple of years earlier. "What should I send her, Greg?" "Pat, send her the whole thing." I did. And she liked it. Eerdmans decided to publish it and call it *AIDS and the Sleeping Church*. So in the midst of CPE I was working with Eerdmans to finalize how the manuscript would be published, including names which needed to be changed and permissions to use names where I had addresses for surviving family members who were willing to have their names used.

In my final CPE unit I needed to design an advanced project. I decided to offer a six-week, evening Spiritual Questing group in a small conference room at St. John's Hospital. Remembering that two years earlier Sam thought just doing *lectio divina* was too short, I brought this problem to my supervisor as I planned the project. Liz suggested adding a weekly reflection question. She recalled liking those at community meetings when she was a nun. I also added a time of sharing and brief guided relaxation at the beginning of each meeting.

I phoned Doug Green, the director of AIDS Care, about this project, and asked if he would help advertise it. He did better than that, he personally pulled together a group of seven and committed to be part of it himself.

The first night of the group, January 4, 1995, it was raining hard, which delayed some of the men, but all seven showed up—in this unfamiliar location, with a woman they didn't know, to do something called spiritual questing. It's a testament to those men that after all the church's rejections, they never gave up on their own spiritual journeys. Sitting around a large conference table, they and the Spirit filled the room.

Once assembled, as a preface to what we would be doing together, I lit a candle in the center of the table to signify the presence of the Spirit, and said, "It is an act of faith that we have come together believing that we incorporate Spirit in us and that we can engage in a spiritual journey." I was putting forward my belief for them, with them, and for myself.

The *lectio* passage we used that first night was not from Scripture but from *A Spiritual Response to AIDS* by Perry Tilleraas:

> Around the country, people are pulling their chairs into circles of hope…because, of course, we can't do this alone. It's too hard, But what is impossible to do alone, is possible with help. The big first step for all of us—whether we are people with AIDS or not, alcoholics and drug addicts or not—is asking for help. Once we do that, the world turns, a path opens up, an empty place in the circle appears, we pull up a chair, and we begin our journey of healing.[3]

They worked well with the passage and with the process, entering into it with seriousness, listening to the passage, meditating on a word or phrase which especially spoke to them, sharing whatever they wished to share, and then offering thoughtful prayers at our conclusion for the person beside them. This was the process I had learned from Norvene and Doug Vest. I added to it having the group join in the "Amen" after each prayer, making each a prayer of the group. Following *lectio,* I handed out two questions for them to think about during the week. The first was, "What name do you give to that which you believe to be sacred?" I felt it was important for me as the leader and for the whole group to know and respect the names people held dear for God. The second question was, "What experience(s) from your childhood or adult life were painful or hurtful and have been most difficult for you to forgive?"

Before we parted, I asked for input from the group about sources for our *lectio* passages. Specifically I wanted to know if they desired to use passages from the Bible. The group decision was to trust me to make good selections for the process and to use biblical material as I saw fit. This felt like an affirmation of their trust in me, a woman most of them had never met before that night.

The weekly meetings went well, with increased bonding among them, as well as ownership of the group. A sign of that came at the end of the fourth meeting, when one participant affirmed the passages we had been using from the Bible, but asked for inclusion of passages from nonscriptural sources. This gave me the opportunity to use a powerful passage from Viktor Frankl's *Man's Search for Meaning*:

> We stumbled on in the darkness, over big stones and through large puddles, along the one road leading from the camp. The accompanying guards kept shouting at us . . . Hiding his mouth behind

3. Tilleraas, *Spiritual Response to AIDS*, 1.

his upturned collar the man marching next to me whispered suddenly: "If our wives could see us now!" And as we stumbled on for miles, slipping on icy spots, supporting each other time and again, nothing was said, but we both knew: each of us was thinking of his (beloved). A thought transfixed me . . . that love is the ultimate and the highest goal to which we can aspire . . . The salvation of humanity is through love and in love.[4]

Love had been a huge issue for all of these men and they worked well with the passage, including one man speaking of his struggle to see love for himself, for another, and God's love as unified. They could strongly identify with "stumbling in the darkness," and "supporting each other time and again."

The sixth and final meeting came quickly for all of us. I prepared the table that night with an individual votive candle at each participant's place. When we began and I had lit the central candle, I invited each of them to light their candles. The *lectio* passage was from C. G. Jung's *Memories, Dreams, and Reflections*:

> About this time I had a dream which both frightened and encouraged me. It was night in some unknown place, and I was making slow and painful headway against a mighty wind. Dense fog was flying along everywhere. I had my hands cupped around a tiny light which threatened to go out at any moment. Everything depended on my keeping this little light alive . . . Though infinitely small and fragile in comparison with the powers of darkness, it is still a light, my only light.[5]

These men were in that situation, trying to maintain hope, trying to stay alive with AIDS. Trying to carve out a place for themselves in society. At the end of the meeting I invited them to take their individual candles home as a reminder of their confidence in themselves, confidence in each other, and the presence of the sacred in each of them. For six weeks, they had been together, and with me, in their work to claim their spiritual journey. In our informal wrap-up time, they let me know they did not want the group to end. I said I'd be interested in continuing the group if a meeting place could be found. I was about to finish my fourth unit of CPE and this conference room would no longer be available.

---

4. Frankl, *Man's Search for Meaning*, 96.
5. Jung, *Memories, Dreams, and Reflections*, 87–88.

10

Another Step in a New Career

A place for the group to meet. Check that one off. Doug Green wanted to continue Spiritual Questing as an AIDS Care program. When I finished CPE on February 23rd, there was barely a pause before Doug contracted with me to continue it at their facility in downtown Ventura. After years now of immersion in the AIDS-affected community I was feeling truly summoned. In March, the whole Spiritual Questing group reassembled along with our first female participant.

The space they were renting in a historic building, which used to be the Bard Hospital, included a small meeting room. It didn't take long before the Questers and the friends they were bringing could barely fit in the space. Doug was negotiating to lease a Craftsman house on Palm Street, but moving our group there was a ways off.

Reverend Phyllis Tyler-Wayman was the new pastor at College United Methodist Church in Ventura. We knew each other from when she had served a church near where I had lived in Inglewood, California. I asked Phyllis about meeting space and she gave me an enthusiastic yes. So the group began meeting in that church's education building. We had a small room with sofas and folding chairs and a coffee table for our votive candles, which had become a regular part of every gathering.

I would arrive early and say hi to Ellen Pearson—the church secretary, usually the only person in the building—would get the lights on in our room, and set things up. I wanted it to look welcoming when the group arrived.

We had two new members, Matthew and Ed, living with advanced AIDS, which was taking a toll on their bodies. Both men had a serious interest in their spiritual lives. Ed was, I believe, living at his parents' home. They were very supportive of him. Matthew was living at Christopher House, a two-story historic house which had been purchased and rehabbed by AIDS activists in the community. Its purpose was safe, pleasant, afford-able housing for people living with AIDS. There was a shared kitchen and living room.

All too soon, Christopher House, which was intended as long-term housing for ambulatory people, became a hospice setting. That's what hap-pened for Matthew. He had been in Spiritual Questing a short time when he became too ill to continue. I visited him regularly at Christopher House.

Ed and Matthew died close to the same time and left us as a group grieving. I had gotten to know both of these men and needed to deal with my own grief. I guessed that focusing the loss might help others in the group as well. They were all facing the same fate. I proposed to them that we dedicate one of our meetings for a service of remembering. One of our female members told me she would skip it because she didn't do funerals. The others agreed to it. When the night of the remembrance meeting came they all showed up (including the woman). Our members were joined by Ed's parents and Dr. Patty Temple, a beloved chiropractor who volunteered her services with patients, and a man who had been close to Matthew. I brought my CD player and had placed a white column candle and the vo-tives on the coffee table.

I opened the gathering with the lights out and only the tall candle burning and began, "In this darkness we light candles, symbols of the pres-ence of the Spirit which continues from age to age. The spirit which was present in Matthew and in Ed was one with God's Spirit and is present with us and in each of us, also." A playing of Rutter's "Requiem Aeternam" helped move us into our heart space. Then I invited them to offer brief prayers of thanksgiving for particular gifts they had received from Ed or Matthew, and after each remembrance to light a votive candle. When they finished, all the candles were lit.

Our remembrances were followed by prayer:

"May we live with gratitude for the gifts they brought to life. And may we be grateful for whatever days are given us, mindful of every moment and the sacred content each moment may carry. Keep love and hope alive in your life. They are sacred and they continue."

Then we passed God's peace to each other.

Writing liturgy was new for me. It seemed the Spirit was guiding me as I shared my belief that God was/is present in us and with us. This service of remembrance was my first opportunity to sacramentalize grief with a group of clients and caregivers.

Spiritual Questing met at College United Methodist until AIDS Care moved into the Palm Street house with a spacious living room we could use.

Facilitating two groups a week (Spiritual Questing and the family support group) was encouraging, but could not be called a job. I continued exploring all options for a position. I had resumed my weekly visits at the Immunology Clinic. Dr. Prichard and I were in conversation about a salaried position for me there as a chaplain. He seemed very much on board with the idea, but faced huge obstacles. The hospital had never had a chaplaincy position and didn't see why this weekly outpatient clinic should have one. The fact that young men, and some young women, were desperately ill and dying was not, apparently, a convincing reason to have a chaplain.

St. John's Hospital paying me to facilitate the family support group became a problem and they were thinking about discontinuing the group. Doug offered to pick up my pay for the group if St. John's would continue contributing the space. They agreed to that.

I was deeply affected by the weekly evening meetings of the family support group. In November of 1995, I wrote the following in my journal:

> I feel like I'm in a war zone, the wounded, dead, and dying all around me. Frantic and grieving family members, lovers, friends calling, paging, gathering, trying to make it through.
>
> This morning was a funeral mass for Dan. His mother and sister were with him to the end. His mother, Judy, planned the service. It was a mix of comfort and anger. The scripture: Judge not that you be not judged, spoke of her fierce loyalty not only to her non-gay son, but to all the sons and daughters and mothers and fathers and lovers and friends out in the trenches of this war that has no face in the United States.
>
> They are angry and grieving. Their anger is a place to put the grief and frustration. Why hasn't the nation mobilized, they ask? And I ask with them. The skeletal bodies are everywhere, racked with pain from the most unbelievable diseases that take them over when their immune systems are finally gone. But these thousands of bodies, people, are invisible to most of the nation. How can it be?

Nineteen ninety-five was the final year AZT alone was the main medication being offered to AIDS patients. Nineteen ninety-six would be the turnaround year when a protease inhibitor was added to a combination that was called "the cocktail." But patients would still be dying into 1996, sometimes only months after diagnosis.

In February and March, I was in frequent contact with Sandra De-Groot, the acquisitions editor with Eerdmans Publishing, as we worked on finalizing the journal manuscript I had kept during my year as an AIDS Project Los Angeles volunteer. Sandra was in touch with artist John Swanson about using his art for the book. I was thrilled to have John's art on the book.

In October, it was published as *AIDS and the Sleeping Church*. The cover art was from his painting, "Agony in the Garden." Sandra had arranged for Henri Nouwen and Joan Chittister, OSB, two well-known religious writers, to write comments for the back of the book. Rev. Dr. James Lockwood-Stewart, a respected United Methodist clergyman, who had been my pastor a few years earlier, agreed to comment for the cover as well. My friend Reverend Chris Glaser, by now an in-demand writer and speaker in the gay and religious community, wrote the foreword. In the back of the book was a section of prayers. Sandra had needed a few more pages of copy and I shyly sent her a few prayers I had written, and she liked them! Two were prayers I wrote for mothers in the family support group. There was one page of the breath prayers I had written for Sam. There was a prayer written by Matthew, the man who had attended Spiritual Questing until he was bedridden. The book, with his prayer in it, came out shortly after his death. There were several wonderful poems which friends contributed: one from the Reverend Perry Wiggins, and two from my poet friend, Ivy Dempsey. Cover to cover, I felt held by these friends.

When the book came out, Doug Green put on a reception at AIDS Care's new location in the Craftsman house in downtown Ventura. About two blocks away, on Main Street, the independent Ventura Bookstore featured *AIDS and the Sleeping Church* in the window—for a year. Timm Herdt, a columnist with the *Ventura County Star*, somehow arranged for a full-page commentary with a big picture of the book and quotes from it. Two clients from the clinic mounted that page and gave it to me. It was a heady time.

11

An Actual Position!

By January 1996, Doug had secured funding for a half-time position and hired me as AIDS Care's first chaplain with a mental health twist. At my suggestion, this first grant was not for my work as a chaplain, (religious work I knew was harder to fund) but to replicate a mental health program I was acquainted with in Los Angeles that offered mental health providers free continuing education training in psychosocial issues for people with HIV/AIDS in exchange for their doing pro bono work with HIV clients. During January, with help from Cecil, I established a good list of area therapists interested in training and serving in this way. I was excited about the opportunity to set up this program, knowing it could help our clients. The plan was I would set up the trainings and would have a single intake visit with interested clients to suggest one or two therapists for them from our list of prepared volunteers.

When Doug had been hired to lead AIDS Care, there had been a small staff. A couple of years later, under Doug's leadership, the staff had grown to include two case workers, a volunteer coordinator, and an experienced administrative person handling accounting and personnel matters. At that time it was an all-female staff except for Doug. He gathered the staff one morning each week for a staff meeting. Just after I was hired and before I had moved into my office, Doug invited me to the meeting.

In the course of that first staff meeting it became clear that one of the women, the volunteer coordinator, had been discussing me with one of the case managers. They were sitting next to each other and brought up to Doug that all the deaths were taking a toll on them psychologically and they thought they should have the benefit of some counseling and, looking at me, they stated emphatically that it wouldn't be with me. Their antipathy shook me, but I rallied and offered to look into pro bono counseling with someone from our volunteer therapist list and said I would report back the next week.

At next week's meeting I reported that I had found a female psychologist who would see any member of our staff without charge and with complete confidentiality. I handed out her business cards to the staff. All they needed to do was phone her and identify themselves as AIDS Care staff and they could be seen for multiple visits free of charge. A year later, I asked this therapist if any staff had ever contacted her. She said no, leading me to think those staff complaints had been less about wanting counseling and more about wanting to diss me, for reasons I can only guess at. My time of euphoria had been brief.

12

In the Exurbia of Outpatient Chaplaincy

I set up my office in a small, gabled room on the second floor. There was a desk with a donated computer on it, but no printer. I added some second-hand furniture: a little love seat (nothing larger would fit) on one wall and an upholstered chair with a narrow side table on another wall. Under the gables was a large double-sash window through which I could see the beautiful old San Buenaventura Mission just across a parking lot. Above the love seat I hung a painting from our house of a ship in a harbor. Over my desk I hung my clinical Pastoral Education Certificates of Completion and an award I received from UCLA Medical Center for outstanding service as chaplain on-call the night of the January 1994 earthquake. I was ready to work.

A few months after I started, the tiny, ancient computer they had assigned to me blew its brains out. I probably had demanded too much of it. Another better computer was donated and delivered. I bought a new printer for home and brought my old one to work. Our son, Bruce, came to the office, loaded on the programs I needed and my files, which blessedly I had kept backed up, and hooked up the printer. He arrived with his toddler and sat down to work at my desk. While he was downloading files and amiably watching the toddler he took care of a phone call he needed to make. I marveled that nothing rattled him and his attention could be on these several tasks with no drop-off in effectiveness. Soon everything was done and with my profuse thanks, he and the grandbaby left.

Most of the client action took place downstairs where the two case managers had their offices along with that of the volunteer coordinator. Also, downstairs at the rear of the building was our food pantry where clients came for bags of groceries. My office was upstairs near Doug's large office and our administrator's work area. This meant when I was working at my desk I was completely removed from people coming in to register as clients or coming for services. I was there at my desk a lot of the time preparing for the first mental health training we would be offering as soon as we could and for the weekly Spiritual Questing group.

In addition to being invisible to most of the clients who were coming and going, I was struggling to integrate this position, and myself personally, into the agency's staff and procedures. I missed the well-defined place of chaplaincy I had experienced at the hospitals where I had trained. In those settings, chaplains had clear and accepted roles, procedures for writing chart-notes that would be read by nursing staff or doctors, and there was an expectation that chaplains would visit new patients to assess their spiritual needs.

None of that was, of course, set up when I began at AIDS Care. My relationships within the staff took shape. I got to know the other case manager, Ana Vargas, a quiet woman who was studying for ministry in the Metropolitan Community Church. We had a mutually supportive relationship. I missed her when she left to take a church position. The originally hostile case manager warmed up to me and, in fact, found me useful when distraught clients or family members showed up in her office. One day she came running up the stairs and urgently asked me to come down to her office. A man with HIV was there, distraught, crying uncontrollably, and making statements about ending it all. I didn't know the man and he was not an AIDS Care client, so I had no information about him.

I hurried downstairs and found him sitting in her rocking chair sobbing. I knelt down in front of him trying to get some idea of what was causing his distress and wanting to comfort him. Finally he was able, through his sobbing, to speak of what had so disturbed him—an extended traumatic experience that had gone on for eight years. He kept mentioning that his neck and head were hurting. It appeared to me he was having difficulty getting his breath. I checked with him on that but did not get a clear response. I asked if I could massage his shoulders and lead him through a guided visualization. He nodded yes.

I stood behind him and gently massaged his shoulders and guided him through progressive relaxation. Gradually his sobs subsided and then stopped. We entered into a guided visualization of a beautiful and safe place where he was met by a figure which brought him a comforting message.

At the close of the visualization, I reminded him that he could always return to that place of beauty and could request the figure come to reassure and comfort him. I spent ten or fifteen minutes more with the man, who now seemed calm, but fatigued. He free-associated for a few minutes. Then I checked with him on where he lived, whether he felt safe driving home, what he planned to do when he left, and who, if anyone, would be at his home when he arrived there. When I was satisfied that he was not suicidal and had plans for something pleasant to do and expected his parents, who loved him, to be at the house, I accompanied him to the front door, gave him my card and said goodbye.

I felt good about the encounter. I had been able to call upon my training to calm the man and return him to his sources of love. But once he had left the house I had a rush of questions. Where should I be recording my encounters? With whom should I interact about them? If he had been a client of the agency would I include a chart-note in a client file and, if so, for what purpose? I was trained to be part of a healthcare team. How does that translate to this social service setting? I was in the exurbia of outpatient ministry.

I developed a brief spiritual assessment questionnaire to be part of the new client intake process. The questionnaire included the question of whether they or someone close to them might be interested in a support group and if so, what kind? It also gave new clients an opportunity to indicate if they had a desire to speak with AIDS Care's spiritual support person. Several had recently indicated that they wanted to speak with me. Those were passed on to me to follow up with, but these new clients were sometimes hard to reach and their interest in meeting me seemed to diminish after they left the premises.

We revised the procedures so that new clients could meet me and other program staff while they were in the house for intake. It was not a perfect plan since I was only in the office twenty-four hours a week at that point, but it was a step toward integrating chaplain services into AIDS Care's overall program.

During most of the first five months I felt overwhelmed by particularities. *Where is the name of that woman I spoke with? I've got to remember to call her. Did I leave that blue spiritual support questionnaire with the client's name on it out on my desk where it could be seen? I left one message for a woman who marked that she wanted to speak with me. Should I keep pursuing it or is the ball in her court?*

I wrote at the time: "I long for the order I experienced in developed chaplain services departments. But AIDS ministry was my chaplaincy goal and here I am with who I am and what I know. God's gift to me is the chance to do this work."

One day, soon after I started the job, I was sitting at my donated computer trying to conceptualize goals and objectives for this unique chaplaincy position in a social service agency. The computer screen was blank. I looked up at my CPE certificates on the wall before me and thought of my supervisors, particularly Karen Schnell, who had helped, trained and encouraged me. I wanted to call Karen and ask, "What do I do now?" But they had done their job and now it was up to me. I sat looking at my certificates and wept. And then I told myself, "You've been trained as a chaplain, and called to this work, so pull yourself together and do it."

AIDS Care had joined the AIDS National Interfaith Network, where the director was Ken South. I had met Ken in Washington, DC, and had seen him again at their national meeting in Los Angeles in October 1995. With my new book out, he had asked me to be a speaker at that meeting. I felt a relationship with Ken, so I phoned him to see if he could help me in how to develop this new ministry. I described our agency and asked if there were any models for anything like this. He said no.

Seeing that it was up to me to figure out, I started reviewing what my training had taught me which could guide me in shaping a chaplaincy program in this secular setting with about a hundred and fifty ongoing clients spread geographically across Ventura County. Active listening, of course, came to mind. I also was remembering a learning module on spiritual assessment. I had found it electrifying at the time because it came close to providing objective measures for planning one's ministry. I dug out my notes. The module was called "Assessing Religious Needs," and religious needs were defined as "any human need viewed in the light of belief or faith in God." Working in a secular setting, I would, of course, define religious in the broadest possible terms. The presenter had been Reverend Janet Humphreys, the Director of Chaplain Services at UCLA Medical Center. My notes from the session just included a long list of possible religious or spiritual needs. More information was probably offered in the next unit, after I left. I phoned Janet Humphreys to ask for more help on how to meet those needs. She gave me a great phone consultation. I have the single sheet of notebook paper on which I quickly jotted notes from our conversation concerning experiences of brokenness and the need for reconciliation, concerning isolation and opportunities for community and intimacy, and concerning despair and hope.

She talked to me about the healing effects of a heightened sense of self-worth and self-esteem; the importance of a renewed sense of meaning and purpose; of awareness of God and noticing grace at work. She talked about people needing to express fear, guilt, and anger, and the need for solace. And she spoke about the place of pastoral counseling and, possibly, referral.

These were not entirely new ideas for me, but having all that laid out on one page helped me move from disordered, scattered thinking to a sense of knowing where I was going. I digested the information, making it available without conscious effort and without needing to find the file folder. This grounding for recognizing and meeting spiritual needs became the basis for every planning decision and every pastoral encounter.

13

Discovering Celtic Spirituality

Have you ever traveled into the interior of Alaska and been lucky enough to catch some views of sacred Denali, the highest mountain in the United States? It is most often obscured by clouds. We made that journey and were lucky to have several sightings.

It was like that for me in catching glimpses of the sacred as I learned of the ancient practices of Celtic Christianity, which were nearly obscured by time and patriarchal political choices. Cecil and I drove up to Santa Barbara to hear Esther de Wall give a lecture on Celtic spirituality. Cecil and I both have Scotch/Irish forebears and were interested in learning about some of the oldest spiritual practices of the Celtic people.

A year or two later, John Philip Newell published *Listening for the Heartbeat of God*, his book on the history of Celtic spirituality. I read it all the way through, and then read it again. The book gave me the ancient family names and their stories of defying darkness, sin, and division to proclaim a message of love, unity, justice, and joy.

I learned that among Celts, women could, and did, have co-standing with men as leaders. That made me happy. Also, the early teacher Pelagius understood infants were born with the image of God. They were not sullied by their origins in sexual intercourse, Pelagius argued, since human sexuality is a gift from God.

These Celtic Christians Newell wrote about gave me theological forebears. His book connected me with ancient roots for a ministry of inclusion and wholeness.

Some years later, Cecil and I attended three different seminars with John Philip Newell—two of them with his wife, Ali—and were enriched by Celtic spirituality for today. I especially love the chants we learned that help move us through our days. They are brief verses from the Bible set to wonderful, short melodies. These chants carry forward the ancient Celtic practices of spoken and sung prayers and chants incorporated by Celtic Christians into their daily lives. Now the chants have become embedded in our own daily lives. (You can find recordings of these present-day chants and Newell's prayers on his website, www. heartbeatjourney.org. I recommend them.)

14

Blessings which Sustained Me

This early period of development of my chaplaincy work was, beyond denying, difficult. But there were blessings that helped me keep going. Foremost, perhaps, was Doug Green's support and affirmation of both my work and me. Doug introduced me to everyone around town as "his chaplain." (Years later he told me he did that because he wanted people to know AIDS Care was attending to clients' spiritual needs.) His affirmations helped me claim my new work identity.

At a deeper level, Doug and I were simpatico from the start, and when I began working at AIDS Care, we were a support to each other. Men we knew and cared about were dying. We both knew we needed to take time, even just a few focused minutes, to grieve these losses. For me, not grieving was the one thing which could send me into a tailspin. Unacknowledged grief has a way of hanging out by the door and then bursting in with something inappropriate. Doug and I developed an informal practice. If either one of us needed a few minutes of special grief time, we would meet, usually in his office. He would shut the door and we would turn his two office chairs toward each other and sit with our fingers lightly touching each other's (Doug contributed that practice), identify the loss we were feeling, and be in silence for a few minutes. We might sometimes speak of particular qualities or memories of the person who had died. Having this practice available was a great blessing.

Doug continued participating in the weekly Spiritual Questing group. Doug was himself a gifted small-group leader, so I suggested that he join me as a co-leader of the group and he accepted that offer. His presence in the group—as a gay man, a leader in the community, and someone people were drawn to—cannot be underestimated, particularly as I was trying to carve out a positive place in the AIDS-affected community.

Cecil was a blessing in more ways than I can enumerate. Cecil was, himself, working hard developing a private practice in Ventura. Still, he managed to support and encourage me, listening enthusiastically to my stories. At a very practical level, he was a great help with the mental health program. As a clinical psychologist who had been networking with others in his field, he had identified some therapists who might be interested in our pro bono program. He also set up my database programs to keep track of the therapists who were seeing clients and the clients being seen. I became proficient with these computer programs, thanks to his help.

There was a gay Latino couple I had gotten to know at the Immunology Clinic. They had been active with the Imperial Strawberry Court, a gay philanthropic organization. One of the men, Jorge, had died and his partner had started coming to the family support group. The partner was involved in planning their annual gala to be held in the ballroom of a large hotel in Oxnard. This was to be a dinner program with music and dancing, where everyone would be dressed in evening attire and some of the attendees would be beautifully dressed in drag. The planning committee invited me to attend and to offer an invocation. I believe it was the first time they had ever asked someone to do this. The invitation was an honor. The night of the event I got dressed up and joined these gay friends for the evening. This was another opportunity for me to put into words my theological perspective on God's presence wherever love and compassion are expressed. Here's the invocation I offered:

> God of all goodness we ask for your presence here with us, and sense that your Spirit already is present:
>
> Present in the goodness of all who are gathered here. Present in your caring about others. Present in your work to raise money to meet needs in the community. And especially present tonight in our memories of Jorge.
>
> May this special occasion express your goodness. May it express a joy and reverence for life and a confidence that those who have gone before us stay with us in spirit.
>
> We ask this in your Many Names. Amen.

Other clients' positive reception of me as a chaplain helped me further integrate and shape this new professional identity.

God delivered more encouragement in the fall of that first year when I was honored as one of two alumnae of the year from Immaculate Heart College, where I had received my bachelor's degree. This was a special thrill for me in several ways. First and foremost, it had taken me so long to get that B. A., when I was forty-six years old. I had gotten married at nineteen and managed to finish only two more semesters before I became pregnant. A couple of moves to remote places intervened. Then for years I took one class at a time until I was forty-five and went all-in to finish at Immaculate Heart College. They facilitated a personalized program to help me finish with a writing major.

With the publication of *AIDS and the Sleeping Church* and, I think, my work in AIDS ministry, our friend Candace Peterson-Kahn, a fellow IHC graduate, put my name forward. Pat Reif, PhD, a professor at the college who had been a colleague in social justice ministry, presented the award to me.

These blessings sustained me during that first year as AIDS Care's chaplain. And they were needed. Besides the challenges of developing a chaplaincy program, there were so many patients dying. It took an emotional toll. In May 1996, I started keeping a journal. Many of the entries referred to the weekly family support group I was continuing to facilitate at St. John's Hospital.

On June 6th, I wrote:

> I feel worn out—shell shocked, really. After a long work day and some complex relationship issues at work, I went to the family support group. It turns out that three women in the group have children near the end and those children are spread all over the place.
>
> One woman's son is in a hospital in Santa Monica. He's in a locked unit, because of his dementia, apparently. She wants to see his face and to say again how much she loves him and that she would never abandon him. But her access to him is blocked right now. Her mother's heart is wrung.
>
> Chris, a faithful member of the group, didn't show up. She sent word that her son is in a hospital in the San Fernando Valley. He is very ill. None of us can imagine how he can go on much longer. When I got home, I called information for the number of that hospital and phoned, but Chris was not there. The nurse told me she knows the patient very well and he is seriously ill. I reached Chris at her home.

Another member of the group is traveling to see her daughter. We got word that her daughter is desperately ill. The daughter has said she will take her own life. I don't know how the mother is processing the progressive illness nor the anticipated suicide.

How do I accompany these women and the people who are important to them?

June 8

I was sitting in a coffee house with my friend Chris Glaser. He had stopped in Ventura to visit me for an hour on his way to Santa Barbara to lead a retreat. I was telling him what a joy it is to be able to see my youngest grandchild often, little two-year old Evan. Suddenly I began to cry. Chris asked why the tears. These were tears for the mothers and grandmothers whose loved children are dying, sometimes away from their sight. He got up from his seat and held me. What a blessing to have a friend who can just receive the sadness and accompany me.

June 30

I dreamt about planes crashing in my neighborhood. There were three altogether. Each one was a different kind of plane and crashed in a separate location. Each time I was on the ground looking up and saying, That plane is going to crash.

I think the planes may symbolize the children of the three mothers in my group.

15

Spiritual Accompaniment

In June 1995, Sharilyn Steketee sent me an invitation to preach at a Sunday service for the Metropolitan Community Church. MCC is a gay-founded denomination which continues to serve the LGBTQ community. When she invited me, my book, *AIDS and the Sleeping Church,* had not yet come out so I was known professionally at that church through my work as chaplain at the once-a-week Immunology Clinic. But on a personal level, I had made friends in the congregation. Their invitation carried an unspoken acceptance of my three years of presence in the gay/lesbian/transgender community.

My sermon that summer at MCC was on Luke 4:16–30. Luke tells us that following Jesus' baptism and time of reflection in the desert he began his ministry. In this passage he was back in his home synagogue where he was invited to read the Scripture and comment. Jesus' remarks clearly identify the coming of God's kingdom, with calling back into community those who were being left out: poor women who had lost status when they beame widowed or divorced; strangers; the ill and deformed; and others who were in some way marginalized. The mission he was announcing was rooted in the long-recognized, although at that time neglected, Jewish traditions of compassion and hospitality as expressions of love of God and neighbor.

Jesus' inclusivity as demonstrated in gospel stories became one theme I regularly included when invited to speak or preach. Jesus' good news had central relevance to the work I had taken on.

A linked theme in my preaching was accompaniment. I had been shaped by the National Farm Worker Ministry's model of ministry based on solidarity with farm workers struggling for justice, entering into their experience, and traveling the road with them.

The term "accompaniment," however, came from the 1980s, back in Los Angeles. At that time, many of us were involved with Central American refugees fleeing the wars of repression in El Salvador and from the contras in Nicaragua. We were seeking ways to offer hospitality and support. Groups in the U.S. began taking sometimes risky journeys of accompaniment in which Americans would accompany Central Americans into war zones. It was a way for Americans to experience first-hand what Central Americans were suffering.

I borrowed the idea and the term "accompaniment" to use in my work in the AIDS-affected community. Accompaniment requires commitment to those you are accompanying. It offers presence as an expression of commitment to justice. I brought this concept to people when I was asked to speak.

The publication of *AIDS and the Sleeping Church* in the fall of 1995 gave me visibility among some clergy in the area. The book had been published by Eerdmans, a respected religious publisher specializing in scholarly works for clergy. Mine was the first in a new line of books. Eerdmans' reputation and reach were significant in bringing my AIDS journal to the attention of clergy who were looking for a way to raise the topic of AIDS in their congregations, and to end the silence which had been so prevalent in churches. The publication of the book along with my position as a chaplain presented them with an opportunity to bring someone from outside the congregation to speak about ministering to people with AIDS. I embraced these opportunities to speak about our clients and to talk about ways to support people with HIV/AIDS and those who loved them.

Several denominations were encouraging programming for AIDS Awareness Month, which was observed each October. Most of my speaking opportunities were clustered in October.

This outreach was slow going, but the list of churches in the area where their own members touched by AIDS felt supported, and where our clients might feel welcomed, gradually grew.

Titles I was using for my sermons were, "Walking Each Other Home," "Their Journey and Mine: Grace in the Age of AIDS," and "Spiritual Accompaniment." Just as Americans traveling into Central American war zones had to bulk up their inner resources, so people like myself and those I spoke to in churches would need to find new capacities within ourselves for this spiritual accompaniment.

When invited to speak, I usually asked to have the following World Council of Churches statement included in the bulletin. It encapsulated much of what I wanted to communicate to congregations:

> The community of the faithful is at its best when it knows itself as a lost—yet found—community, a place where people can share their woundedness and their search for healing. People living in the midst of the AIDS crisis are searching for answers that the silence of prayer and the connectedness with God and others can bring. Prayer can be the Word, spoken and received: the silence of a listener who allows the space for the search, of arms too big to exclude, the tears and the laughter. Prayer can open the heart to a healing that penetrates and infuses our very being. . . . The search for a deeper and more meaningful spirituality on the part of many of those involved in the AIDS crisis is a search for a connectedness, a reconciliation with God, self and others.[1]
>
> World Council of Churches 1986

Much of the American church has kept one foot in Purity Law Land, making clear who is not in the circle of inclusion. Dwelling in that land blinds people to Jesus' ministry of inclusion and compassion. Yet, Jesus was notorious for keeping table fellowship with "sinners." He was called out by religious leaders who were living in Purity Law Land for the infraction of healing on the Sabbath. If you had certain illnesses or conditions, your place in the circle of community was gone. An example was the woman who had been hemorrhaging for many years. She had tried every medical option. When she came to Jesus' attention he told her that her faith had healed her and addressed her as Daughter of Abraham, which meant, "Welcome back to the community."

Illness can still be the named reason to disqualify people for inclusion in faith communities. I personally heard pastors in our area who were living in Purity Law Land claiming AIDS was God's retribution on gay men. I don't know how they worked out the reality of nongay people with AIDS: women, children, and heterosexual men. Most of the AIDS cases in Africa, for example, were and are among nongay people.

The Israelites were reminded time and again by the prophets and teachers to remember they had been slaves in Egypt and God had brought them out of that land into a better land. The World Council of Churches' statement was calling the church to remember itself as a lost and wounded

---

1. "World Council of Churches Executive Committee Statement."

community which should have compassion for strangers and any in need of hospitality. That was a message I wanted to convey.

Speaking in churches was pretty seasonal. The rest of the time I had one hundred and fifty clients to serve, practicing spiritual accompaniment with them. The work kept me returning to the nourishment of God's Spirit for sustenance. The greatest obstacle was not knowing or acknowledging my need at any given moment on any given day. Practicing awareness was like Ironman training for the soul. My daily life covered many terrains, from home and family to the office, from individual work to leading groups. I was trying to be present to so many people in so many situations. But moments of awareness were moments of God's grace pouring over me like cooling water in the desert. What follows is a little story that illustrates the process of going from being emotionally disconnected to living in a state of inner awareness.

In early July, Doug Green and I drove south to Palos Verdes for Kip's memorial service. Chris's son Kip had died in the hospital in Los Angeles, and the service was being held at the Wayfarer's Chapel, a little glass jewel set on the palisades overlooking the Pacific Ocean. It was a long drive and we were a little late. We ended up sitting in the back row. I couldn't see Chris or anyone else I knew except Terry, my friend from the family support group. Terry was tall so I could see him, but he was sitting way down toward the front. I felt isolated and emotionally disconnected during the service.

When the service was over, Doug and I were standing near the back waiting for Chris. I turned around and on the wall next to me I saw the quilt panel friends had made for Kip. In the center was his birth date, December 26, 1957. That's the same birth year as our daughter, Mary. Identification with the loss of a child caught me just as Chris arrived at the back of the chapel. We hugged and my tears were released. Grace was in knowing where the tears came from.

I had daily spiritual practices to help center me in sacred Spirit. While the three mothers in the family support group were anticipating their children's deaths, I had been lighting three votive candles each morning in my meditation time. Now all three of those loved people had died. I put away the three votive candles and returned to the simplicity of the one candle I lit each day. My friend and colleague, Christina Fernandez, had given the candle to me when I completed my fourth unit of clinical pastoral education. It was a slender oil candle, clear glass, with pale pink oil and a wick. It burned with a steady flame that did not flicker.

I started a new ritual using the catalogue from a powerful art exhibit. On the first of July, I had taken my daughters, Mary and Ruth, into Los Angeles to see Judy Chicago's art installation, "The Dinner Party," which was set up in a large room with a great dinner table in the form of a triangle, with thirty-nine handcrafted china plates commemorating female spiritual leaders, artists, poets, writers, and advocates for women. Each plate was set on a hand-stitched runner that spoke of the society which encroached on each woman. The goblets and utensils were identical at every place setting, a metaphor for how societies treated each woman the same no matter how extraordinary each was. The triangular table was set on polished tiles on which the names of nine hundred ninety-nine other notable women were recorded.

Mary and Ruth and I had spent several hours in the room filled with people, all of us hushed, bringing our deep respect for these forebears who had lived with courage. When we were leaving I bought the exhibit book with a page showing each of the memorial place settings.

My new morning ritual was to hold that book of color illustrations in my lap. Each morning began by opening to a different photograph remembering a woman in history who had brought her gifts, whatever the risks or circumstances. Then I would call on the strength of these women to enter into my own spirit.

We can do spiritual accompaniment if we don't carry the illusion that we have solutions to what we see as the "other's" problems. I encountered this in working with some of our clients with active drug and alcohol addictions.

I had met Ben in the hospital just after he was diagnosed. He was twenty-one and had come in for surgery and found out he was HIV-positive. He had been a high school athlete who had experimented with drugs and was an alcoholic. His mother had been killed when he was a child and he had been raised by an aunt with older kids who had exposed him to alcohol and drugs. He had never recovered from the traumatic loss of his mother and used drugs and alcohol to mask his sorrow.

Ben would come to see me at AIDS Care from time to time. And sometimes I would see him on the street, usually drunk.

The morning of August 13, 1996, I was expecting him at my office. I made this journal note:

I'm preparing to meet with Ben and I feel tense. Where is that tension coming from? It is coming from my hope to succeed in helping him out of his dark despair, the pit of grief that has contributed to his alcoholism.

Give this up, Pat, this hope of rescue. The best service I can offer will spring from staying with my feelings. I feel a sense of waste that this young, bright athletic person is caught in the slew of despondency. How often has he been through recovery programs? How many hours has he already spent with his drug and alcohol counselor?

I believe unresolved grief underlies his alcoholism. It is mainly grief from childhood over the murder of his mother—a crime that was never solved. Last week he told me he had just been served with a ticket for public drunkenness while walking through downtown Ventura. He expressed contempt for the ticket. He said, "Why are the police wasting time giving me a ticket for drinking? They should have spent their time finding who murdered my mother."

I can, perhaps, help him with resolving his grief. But I must not be invested in succeeding. My success will be holding whatever happens to Ben in a sacred place of care and acceptance.

He may be drunk right now on the streets and not even come this morning. But he was invited.

My only success with Ben over the years was imprinting in him, drunk or sober, that he was unconditionally cared for. When I say it was my only success with him, I should perhaps say it was a success for me. Over and over again I needed to offer him love without expectation. I was not his drug counselor, I was not his parole officer. I was his chaplain. I was his spiritual companion.

A couple of weeks later I had a late-afternoon call at the office. I was about to go home for an hour to eat and rest before the family support group started. The call was from a client who had asked for and gotten a referral for psychotherapy. He was furious. His voice shook with emotion. He had felt hurt by an interaction with someone in the therapist's office who had, probably inadvertently, interacted with our client in a way that was wounding to him.

The telephone felt hot with the heat of his anger as the first blasts came across to me. I tried to sort out what had happened, tried to listen with compassion. The client had been through so much. We stayed together on the phone until the molten lava of his fury had flowed a distance and begun to cool. Some equilibrium was restored, thanks be to God.

I left the office for the short drive home before going to the group. Driving along Foothill Road I felt the tension in my body. I began to cry, releasing that tension. The tears seemed to be my response to the brokenness, to the wound our client felt, to the stress I experienced trying to stay with the fury and sort out what had happened. The tears also came in response to the relief I felt since a level of resolution had been reached. Spiritual accompaniment of my client required staying with him through his difficult emotions.

In July, Cecil and I took a much-needed vacation to a favorite place of ours: Ghost Ranch, in northern New Mexico. They had invited me to do a seminar on spiritual healing in the AIDS epidemic, but at the last minute, after we had already arrived, I was told it had been cancelled due to low registration. The upside of the cancellation was that I was able to attend a seminar led by The Reverend Dr. Paul Smith, a gifted pastor from New York.

Dr. Smith invited me during that week to lead an hour on journaling. I read from my journal, *AIDS and the Sleeping Church.* Then I talked about writing as self-care and self-affirmation. Finally, I invited seminar participants to do *lectio* on life (another process I had learned from the Vests), allowing their minds to settle on some incident or interaction during their time at the ranch that had meaning for them, and to write it down.

For two days people were speaking to me about the power of that hour and thanking me. I, in turn, was reflecting on what I could learn from their responses and the responses of other people over the past two years.

When I was doing hospital chaplaincy, I understood myself as capable of brief but comforting and supportive relationships. My AIDS ministry work has required something more of me. In fact, it has brought out more in me.

On July 20th, there at Ghost Ranch, I wrote:

> I'm seeing this morning that everything from my past—every pain, every loss, every hour of therapy, every experience—has a place to be used now. I have gone down into myself, deeper perhaps than I have recognized, toward that taproot. When I am connected with it, I have a grounding for being with people in some more healing way. Thanks be to God.

16

We were Specializing in Grief

In August, I convened the first AIDS Care Grief Group and the first grief group I had ever facilitated. My grief care mentor, Pickens Halt, MFT, had retired and given me her structured grief group materials. Working with a group made better use of my time and promised to provide more support for individual grievers. Nine men and women showed up, most of them strangers to each other and to me. For this first meeting I had planned a process for sharing fairly objective information to give people a chance to get comfortable before sharing more deeply. However, the grief just flowed out, from their lips, their eyes, their hearts. No process could have held it back. In my journal, I wrote:

> We formed a circle and their grief flowed into it. Overflowed its edges. Left us awash in sorrow. We held hands at the end so we wouldn't drift away on the tide. We held hands and in a small voice I called out to them to hold on—to this fragile community we are just now forming—to the gifts the lost ones left behind—to a hope that their grief will have an end.
>
> They left with embraces and brief messages to each other and from me. I did my staff things: close the windows, pull the shades, lock the door. But I kept sighing and my sighs said my heart remained locked on their stories. In the circle I had named them sacred stories. Now I felt the power of the sacred, the passing out of sight of persons loved, passing into the unknown ether. And the final days or moments people had spoken of...*I told him how proud I was of him and the good job he got the last year of his life, the only good job he ever had...I had just put the earphones on for him so he could hear the music of his friend Peter...He died as he had wanted, at home in his momma's arms with his sister by him...*

He had promised he would let us know when he was ready to go and
he kept his promise with a signal of his hand. Sacred stories.

In late September, we held the tenth annual AIDS Candlelight Vigil. It was the first one I had helped plan. Like all the previous ones, it was held in the evening at the downtown park, a square in front of the post office. We had, I think, our biggest turnout to date, over a hundred people. The logistics had been a real headache. We needed a sound system, but there didn't seem to be any place to plug into. Finally, on the afternoon of the event, our volunteers, using the only electrical outlet they could find, set up the sound equipment on the paved area in front of the public bathrooms. So, our speakers had the restrooms as their backdrop, restrooms with folks who were not participating in the vigil going in and out, and flushing, of course.

I made a vow that I would never go through that again. The vigil was going to be indoors in the future. I wanted it in a church but the AIDS-affected community was so skittish about churches. The Church of Religious Science, however, was known as a welcoming place and was just four blocks from the park. The next year, and for several years after, we held it there with fabulous support from the pastor and from members of the congregation, some of whom were lesbian or gay.

After the vigil, participants had a candlelight procession back to AIDS Care for the dedication of four new AIDS quilt panels and then a reception. I journaled about it later that night:

> So many people that I have known and care about, and people who have spoken to me on the phone but I'd not met before or people I have heard about. Conversations. Stories.
>
> Dixie came. She brought mementos in an 8x10 frame. I can't tell you what all was in the frame. My eyes fixed on the obituary clipped from the newspaper. It included a photo of her very handsome son. I noticed he had been born in 1963, a year younger than my youngest child. Dixie was dressed entirely in red, like a living AIDS ribbon.
>
> Jimmy's mother gave me a beautiful red ribbon pin that her sister-in-law had given her. She pinned it on my black suit jacket. She showed me her gold AIDS bracelet. It has Jimmy's name engraved on it. She apologized for not staying in touch. Her husband was with her and I remember when he would sometimes come with Jimmy to clinic.

I had not met Maxine before. I know her brother Jackson. Maxine and I kept trying to have a conversation but would be interrupted by this need and that. You know how it is trying to talk at an event, especially an agency event when you're a staff person. Finally, we stood in the dark part of the entry hall and she related the beauties and burdens of her family's caring for her brother, Joe, through to his death. "We hadn't planned it out," she told me, "we just always told Joe we would be there when he needed us. And we were." Maxine had dropped everything and moved to Atlanta to be with Joe. Their mother came too. And Jackson, my friend from Ventura, took a four month leave of absence from work to be there. He was prepared to leave his job if he had to.

Maxine related the details of her brother's last hours and her insistence on being the one to give him his morphine. She was not going to have even the hospice nurse doing that.

Throughout the conversation I saw people coming and going through the front door, saw them as they came from behind Maxine and passed by. I noticed them but wanted to stay with the story she was relating, to rest into it, give myself over to it. I wanted nothing to be more important at that moment. Who is this woman telling me this remarkable story of love, of commitment to family, of the experience of deep connection that surrounded the final four months of her brother's life?

I had a fleeting memory of Jackson's account of bathing their brother's body and dressing it after he died. The intimacy and the care etches the story in my mind.

Next Morning

In the silence of my morning meditation, scenes and feelings from last evening's Vigil come back to me with a gnawing sense of oughtness. The Vigil went so well, but what more ought I to have done? In the swirl of activity before the Vigil began—meeting with the six readers, giving program notes to the musicians, giving instructions to the candle lighters—I glimpsed the faces of women from the Family Support Group. We have journeyed so far together, week by week by week. I wanted to hold them. Wanted to clearly acknowledge them and what I know of their struggles and losses. A barrier of necessity separated me from them.

Now, the next morning, I cry a little thinking about them: Chris, and Muriel, and Dena, and Shirley, Susan, and Judy, as well as Rusty, and Bill, and Sam, whom I did not see but heard were there. Will they know how much I care about them? Was the Vigil itself an occasion that held them when we could not hold each other? I am trying to release feelings of oughtness, the feeling that I have not done enough.

> I know I have done all that I could. They were at the Vigil with people significant to them. I pray that God's comfort and blessings were available to each person who came. And I pray that I might be accepting of myself and my limits.

In October, I flew to Washington, DC for the National Skills Building Conference for AIDS professionals. I met Doug Green there and Art McDermott, the convener of the Ventura County AIDS Partnership. While we were in DC we went together to see the Names Quilt spread out on the Capitol Mall—all 42,000 panels. It was overwhelming. There was a continuous recitation of the names of the dead. During the hour we were there I heard the name of someone I had known eight years earlier in Los Angeles.

I was staying with friends, a clergy couple, Dean and Jim McDonald. On Sunday, I preached at her church, Chevy Chase, using the story of the prophet Elijah in I Kings 17:8–24, who goes to stay with a poor widow in Sidon, in what is now Lebanon. Elijah goes empty-handed, but he and the widow and her son are able to get through the time of drought together. In spiritual accompaniment, we come to one another empty-handed, bringing only ourselves and our trust in the divine spirit.

"I've had two sons die of AIDS," the caller said simply on the phone. "Do you offer services in Ventura County?" she asked. I inquired how long ago the deaths had occurred and she said one son had died two weeks earlier.

It was a busy day at work. It was just before the AIDS Candlelight Vigil that was coming up on Sunday evening. I'd been finalizing the program, meeting with people, and working on the press coverage. At the end of the day, I got into my car to go home and felt peppy. The radio was tuned to a jazz station. I drove about five miles before I got still. When I was still, what came to mind was, "I've had two sons die of AIDS. One died two weeks ago."

I began to cry.

My sadness could not well up when I had all these other things going on—things I needed to do. Now what I needed to do was stop the car right there on Foothill Road and be still, to feel the sadness and to shed some tears for that woman who had called me that day.

Part of accompaniment was being able to feel the sorrow of others. Without feeling the sadness, I could not hope to help because they would sense my distance and know I was only good for information. I learned, however, that while I didn't need to stay in the sadness, I needed to be able to touch it when it was there.

The woman who called on the 24th called again. "I had a real shock today," she said. She had received an envelope from the Ventura County Hospital. It was addressed to her dead son. She thought it might be a bill left over from July when he was there. She opened it and it was the silver ring she had given to her son.

I was trying to listen closely. "How did it feel to you to have his ring back?" I asked. "Wonderful," she said, "because it meant that I have something else of his now. And I had given it to him."

She had called it a shock and I'm sure it was. But it was a redemptive shock, another link to her son.

One morning in late October, our case manager, Marti, ran upstairs to my office at about 4:30. She was experiencing acute grief anticipating the death of our client, Lydia. Marti was crying and talking about what this client had brought into Marti's life and that it had been her first client, one year earlier.

Marti was sitting in my desk chair turned away from me toward the window. I was sitting on the little sofa where I had been working on something when she rushed in. "How can I bear this?" she asked. "This is too hard. There is no manual. Tell me what to do." Her verbalizations were all ones I had made eight years earlier when I was first involved as a hospital volunteer with AIDS patients. I had not learned any answers, except to trust the need to express grief, and to acknowledge loss.

When Marti burst into my office crying while I was doing other work, I felt some detachment from the drama as she expressed her grief. But after sitting with her, allowing space and silence, allowing my own defenses against the pain to lower, I got in touch with my own grief about Lydia. Some silent tears ran down my cheeks, too.

We all did a lot of crying in those years. I'm remembering one of the early clients I met when I had been an APLA hospital volunteer. Dan was bedbound. At the end of one of my visits he reached for a packet of new white handkerchiefs. He asked me if I cried and I said I did sometimes. Then he handed me one. He knew what I was in for, what we all were in for. But I was committed. I was in the place God had called me to be. We were all crying, but if we held onto each other, we would not be washed away.

17

Reassessing for Ministry

Ministry with real people is never static and it certainly wasn't during the AIDS epidemic. The virus kept adapting, there were political and societal shifts, and treatments became more effective. Our clients experienced these changes.

My friend Teresa Bremer and I were having a phone visit. She was a psychotherapist in Santa Monica, California. She told me she was seeing two men who were living with AIDS. She brought up the huge impact the new protease inhibitors, the "cocktail," were having on her two clients. They were both feeling relatively well on the medications and trying to figure out how to reclaim their lives. Their stories were similar to those appearing in newspapers and magazines, with titles like "An End to AIDS?"

I asked, "What emotional impacts are you seeing?" She noted that one man was experiencing distress as he tried to return to his profession at the same level where he had been when he quit work. The other man was confronting the problem of paying off his credit cards and repairing his credit rating. Living with AIDS is expensive. At that time, the drugs needed to stay alive could cost $20,000 to $30,000 a year, and if you had to go to the hospital that was thousands more. One man told her he had maxed out all his credit cards, figuring that no one cares what kind of credit a dead man has. Now, people living with AIDS were finding out they needed to adjust their plans and their thinking. It looked like they were going to be living with AIDS rather than dying of it.

Most of AIDS Care's clients were in public health programs funded by state and federal money. It was never enough, but it was essential to providing some level of care for people who were no longer able to work and who were without private insurance. Because of these programs clients might not have been dealing with maxed out credit cards or reverse mortgages that they wished they could get out of, but they were faced with other difficult issues. For many clients it was learning to cope with life without drugs or alcohol. They were struggling to live with HIV/AIDS and their doctors and counselors were telling them that their addictions were keeping them from the level of health they could now achieve with the "cocktail."

What a challenge it was for clients with addictions to learn ways to cope without drugs or alcohol! For many it would be the first time in their lives. But if they wanted to live, they needed to scale that mountain. However, drugs and alcohol were never my focus. Others with expertise in addictions were working on that.

My whole focus as their chaplain was to return them to their belovedness. They came into the world beloved, but many had learned a different story after they were abandoned, raped, or found unacceptable because they were gay. My mission was to mirror back to them a new image, an image of one who is valued and loved. With some I was able to help either individually or within the life of a group. With others the mountain was Kilimanjaro and we never got past base camp.

I had altered my route to work because I was looking for Alfred. Alfred had been a full-time volunteer with us. In fact, Doug had him join our weekly staff meetings. But several months into that arrangement, Alfred had disappeared. Heroin had been his drug of choice and we figured he had started using again. It was winter and we all were concerned about him living on the streets.

He had been spotted along Thompson Avenue. Each day, as I took the off-ramp from the 101 freeway and approached Thompson, I would think of Alfred. I thought of him sleeping in the rain and now in the cold. People talk about getting wasted. It's an appropriate term. Alfred was getting wasted. Such a bright and able man, but also injured and grieving. Was it his grief over Bob's death from AIDS that had started this cycle?

I exited the off-ramp, and turned left onto Thompson, driving the two blocks to Palm Street slowly, searching on both sides of the street for a sight of him. As I approached Palm I saw Marti, our case manager, was driving just ahead of me. I think she was looking, too. When we both pulled into the parking lot behind AIDS Care, I told her that I was still looking for

Alfred and she said she was too. I asked her what we should do if we spotted him and she laid out a plan.

Then there was James. When I first met him he was not HIV-positive. What happened? Did he intentionally put himself at risk to be part of the club? Knowing the answer to that was beyond the scope of what I could do and how I could help. I wrote about him in January 1997.

> This week there have been two very depressed clients at AIDS Care, helping out, being with people, trying, I guess, to stay alive. Being HIV+ hangs over them but is not the main cause of their depression.
>
> Today James, 22, was sitting in my office with quiet tears running down his face, saying I shouldn't waste energy worrying about him because he wasn't worth it, and that I should save that energy for others. James has a bad cold and is homeless again.
>
> I told him that I heard how bad he is feeling right now. However, heart-space is not limited. Time is limited, but there is unlimited heart-space and he has some of mine and will continue to do so.
>
> I could see there was no point in trying to get him to do this or that, as bad as he felt. The real problem (besides being homeless) is his devaluing of himself. I told him I had a staff meeting to go to, and as we stood I held him for a minute and whispered to him that he is loved.
>
> The Next Day
> This morning James felt much better. He was at the office ahead of me and was at the volunteer desk answering the phones. When I arrived I put my lunch and briefcase down and we talked for a couple of minutes. He reflected on how messed up he was yesterday. I let him know how valuable it is to us to have him volunteering, answering the phones and helping with other tasks.
>
> By afternoon he was physically worse, hacking up a storm. Another regular volunteer came in to answer phones for the afternoon but refused to stay if James was going to be there coughing. Downstairs staff were also concerned for themselves and others. I needed to leave in the middle of the afternoon to do a group in Oxnard. As I was leaving, I spoke to James, expressing concern for his health and that of others and encouraged him to see his doctor, and perhaps get on antibiotics. He looked angry and cold as I spoke to him. I expect he put what I was saying in his

Nobody-cares-about-me basket, which is really his I-don't-care-about-me file.

We had no intercom at AIDS Care, so when Marti wanted my help with an emergency she would run from the front to the back of the house and up the stairs to my office. This time it was Nate on the phone. He was sobbing and asking if I would talk to him. Intensive active listening on the phone is hard work, what with listening for the underlying message, mirroring back to be sure I got it, and trying to get a sense of what was at the core of the events. It took a few minutes to get what had triggered this avalanche of emotion I was hearing. Then, because Nate can get lost in his emotions, I was much more direct than I would normally be: speak with Marti about the money problems; phone your therapist (free through our program) and let her know how you are feeling today. Don't despair if you can't connect with her. Know that it has been a positive act of self-care to call and even leave her a message. You can give yourself comfort. You're worth it. You are one of God's creations.

After I hung up, I tried to do this and that and noticed I kept muttering, "Dear God, Dear God." I've learned that's a tip-off that I need to be still and silent. I closed my door and a tear or two welled up in my eyes. It had been such an effort. Like pulling a drowning man to shore—get him onto the beach! Get help! Get those vital signs reestablished! Fifteen or twenty minutes of total attention and then my rubber band went limp.

I sat quietly with attention, noticed the tightness in my chest, and breathed into it. I let myself know what an effort that had been and that I had given it my best.

The protease inhibitors, with their promise of longer life, had an impact on some of our clients which was somewhat veiled from me. Daniel was doing well on the "cocktail." Then he simply stopped taking his medications, got very sick, and died. It was all so quick. I remember Dr. Prichard was angry at how Daniel had sabotaged himself like that. I was baffled.

In Spiritual Questing a couple of our members struggled with staying on the medication regimen. I should have asked more questions about it at the time. These regimens were not easy and I assumed that was the reason. Years later, Art talked to me about his feelings of survivor guilt. So many friends had died. Why should he have this chance to live? I do remember in the group we kept encouraging Art and others to stay on their medications.

Sometimes God's Spirit is at work even when those of us in ministry are clueless.

I was reassessing our long-running family support group. One night, Dena was the only person who came. Actually it was fortunate because she needed the whole hour and a half. Her deaf son, her only child, had advanced AIDS. The doctor told her during the week, "You do know that there's nothing more we can do. Your son will not live to next year." She had known how ill her son was, yet the news was a shock.

Her son was living with her and her husband. She believed he was possessed by the devil. Surely evil seemed to have taken over his life: dementia, drugs, and perhaps post-traumatic stress disorder. He did not have a rational mind.

She and I had been together in this group for how long? Two years? That night I gave her my fullest attention, my best reflective listening, an open heart. With our private time, she brought her questions about a merciful God that would allow her son to suffer so and would bring this long and unrelieved suffering to her. Where did I find the merciful God, she asked? I told her where I saw God's merciful face, and one place was in her, in her continued compassion toward a son who treated her spitefully. "How can good come from this horror?" she asked again and again. We stayed locked together in an intense inspection of these great questions.

In my journal that night, I wrote:

January 23

Is it still Epiphany? Can this beloved woman who was never parented by any trustworthy adult trust that care is there for her and reach out and touch hands that might support her? She is reaching out for me. Can I be trustworthy for her? The group has grown so small. I have shared with the members that we will probably end the weekly meetings. There is only this one member who really needs the meeting at this time.

I feel exhausted, spent. I've even cried a little. They were tears of exhaustion. Now I've enjoyed a quiet supper alone, left-over ratatouille over rice with a thick slice of rich wheat bread and peppermint tea, and the choir of Trinity College, Cambridge singing sacred songs. Barber's "Agnus Dei" especially touched me. I'm slowly recovering.

In mid-February, we held the final meeting of the family support group. It had met weekly for eight years. For the past three I had been the facilitator. I remember one time in CPE describing myself as dogged in pursuit of my goal of AIDS ministry. My supervisor, Elizabeth Cook, rephrased it as "faithful." I was faithful to this group, bringing it the best I had to offer.

The final meeting was a celebration. Former members whose loved ones had died were invited back, as well as Pickens Halt, MFT, who had facilitated the group before me, and Doug Green.

We had food and sat in a circle, recollecting. Three women remembered their first time coming to the group. One recalled having a panic attack upon hearing another mother talking about planning with her son for his funeral, and feeling a need to run out of the room. Another remembered being silent for weeks. A third woman recalled crying through the whole first meeting and how comforted she was by two of the women.

Dena and her husband were there. She believes her son is close to the end. She said the group had been better for her than psychiatry, and that she would miss it. I asked her to talk about how we might continue to support her. It was difficult for her to ask for help. I promised to phone her over the weekend for a report on her son's condition. And I did that.

After the meeting, Chris and Muriel helped carry things to my car. Before we parted, Chris said it felt like the end of an era. She had been there at the beginning of the group eight years earlier when her nephew was diagnosed. She had been part of the group through the years her son Kip was living with HIV, and now she was here at the end.

It was a new time with the introduction of protease inhibitors. I drove away from that final meeting with a sense of completion, but also uncertainty about how to support family members in this new time in which many of their loved ones were feeling much better and had hope for living longer with HIV.

18

Widening Our Reach

Protease inhibitors came just in time to save the lives of many of our clients. In a way it was just in time for me too. Nineteen ninety-seven marked for me six years of cumulative grief. I was, I think, close to burnout. I got into therapy to help me relearn playing and goofing off. And Cecil and I had some couples therapy to help improve our skills at supporting each other. Having fewer deaths, however, was its own therapy. I had been wading through deep waters to get to people who were drowning. Now I had a chance to anchor some footbridges over that River Jordan.

One developing need was to get emotional support services closer to our clients in the eastern part of the county. Our clients in Thousand Oaks and Simi Valley saw they had a chance to live longer and they were asking for support groups and services. Some of my time in '97 and '98 was spent doing just that, expanding our presence into east county.

I was excited about our second mental health training event, which was set to be held at California Lutheran University in Thousand Oaks in September 1997. One of our presenters was Adam Chidekel, PhD. He was the founding director of the Pacific Center for HIV/AIDS Counseling and Psychotherapy, the Los Angeles nonprofit I had modeled our program on. He was my mentor in how to provide pro bono mental health services to people with HIV/AIDS. How did I first meet him? It must have been while I was working with the Education and Research Project in Long Beach. When I started the Mental Health Program at AIDS Care, Adam had been generous in providing me with some phone consultation.

Adam's center, however, had a very different clientele than most of ours. A major problem which had plagued our program in its first eighteen months was no-shows. A client would book a pro-bono appointment with one of our volunteer therapists and then would not show up, or even call. This problem was likely related to clients with substance abuse issues.

I was equally excited about our other presenter, Neva Chauppette, PsyD, who had a specialty in comprehensive HIV services to substance abusers. She ran two mobile clinics in Los Angeles, getting services to that beleaguered population.

This training was available to our continuing therapists and also attracted sixteen new ones, mostly people practicing in East County, two of them bilingual in English and Spanish, a special need we were trying to meet. Counseling was another tool for helping people cope with living with HIV/AIDS, and whatever else life was presenting them.

These sixteen new therapists joined the twenty trained ones the year before in their desire to know more about the specific challenges being faced by our clients. Almost every therapist trained was assigned a client, and through those clients therapists learned the personal side of living with AIDS. One of the therapists told me years later that she cared deeply about the client she had worked with and still periodically saw her. How much were attitudes changed in the Ventura County therapeutic community about HIV/AIDS by this program? I don't know. But thirty-six therapists were more informed and involved than they would have been without the program. So in addition to helping clients, the program made a contribution toward influencing social attitudes in a county that leaned toward being socially conservative.

Some of the psychotherapists who attended our trainings came because they wanted a chance to serve, but they were already way ahead of the curve. One of those was the Reverend Frank Johnson, MFT. He was a retired United Church of Christ clergyman, and a marriage and family therapist in East County. Frank was active at the Simi Valley United Church of Christ, a small, progressive congregation. Frank became a link to that church and a friend and support person for me at that end of the county where I was just beginning to learn my way around.

This church agreed to host a weekly support group for clients which was facilitated by one of our new pro bono therapists. This acted as a much-needed bridge to clients.

I was interested in expanding support for the AIDS-affected community in churches and encouraging inclusivity. Whenever an opening came along I jumped into it. A big opening came when Episcopal Deanery I, a regional body, asked us to conduct their first AIDS Ministry day-long training. It was an opportunity for our staff to teach workshops on prevention issues and socioeconomic needs. In my keynote address, I focused on how to provide spiritual support to clients and those who love them.

I was asked to make presentations on AIDS Ministry at a Lutheran pastors' conference, the Presbyterian Synod of Southern California, and Hawaii's Mission Rally. These invitations came because of the interest and concern of particular people. I was happy to be their ally in increasing understanding of the need for churches to reach out to the AIDS-affected community, and to do that effectively.

When I worked with the farmworker movement, I had learned the importance of giving people a range of ways to help. I adapted that to my work in AIDS Ministry. One outreach I made to churches was asking them to give an annual gift of $150 to pay for a client to attend a spiritual support retreat. I don't remember how many letters I sent out, but in 1997, seventeen churches made contributions which paid the way for thirty-seven clients to attend a weekend retreat at La Casa de Maria, near Santa Barbara.

At the retreat, I distributed a list to the retreatants of the churches that had helped. I wanted to lower our clients' religious-fear barrier. After the retreat I sent a report to each church. This was a way for them to have an embodied view about people with HIV/AIDS: thirty-seven people with HIV/AIDS gathered at a Catholic retreat center for a weekend of spiritual support conducted by a chaplain. In 1997, that news probably created psychological dissonance for some churchgoers. That would be movement in the right direction.

How much did my outreach help change attitudes in the Ventura County religious community? I don't know. But I do know that every church committee that received our request and evaluated it was having a conversation about AIDS in Ventura County. And in the churches that contributed, that item was showing up on the church budget for everyone to see. At that time it was so important to lift AIDS out of the shadows and help church people speak about it with less stigma. AIDS was affecting someone in virtually every congregation. I hope some of those affected people felt supported as a result of our work. That year, $7,500 was donated by churches for our two retreats.

Another outreach was for our observance of AIDS Awareness Month each October. In 1997, I made a second appeal to churches (the first being for retreat scholarships), asking them to put our announcement of the annual Fall Vigil in their bulletins and newsletters. We wanted to reach out to affected families we might not know.

I had learned from similar efforts when I was with the National Farm Worker Ministry about all the ways a request for a bulletin announcement can go astray: it's not addressed to the right person at that church; the secretary is out sick and the letter is lost in a pile of mail; it goes to the pastor who already has too much to take care of, and so on.

This first year I was working on phone follow-up to be sure the letters got to the right person, and I was drowning. I needed help. My daughter Mary called one day to see how things were going. She said she had some time available and could come over and make these phone calls to churches. What a help that was! She was asking them if they had received our bulletin announcement and would they be using it? She kept a record of each call and every outcome, including those to whom she faxed or resent the letter. That year we had our largest attendance at the vigil. This was the one held inside for the first time, at the Church of Religious Science in Ventura. One hundred thirty-five attended.

We were swinging footbridges over the chasm between churches and our clients.

Thank God the number of deaths was falling sharply. Still, clients and people in the wider community were calling asking for help with their grief. I did some grief care over the phone and some in person in my office. The following are two grief stories I recorded in my journal:

April 15, 1997 Tuesday

I was at the office, just getting going on the day today when I was given a call from a woman seeking a group. "Tell me something about yourself, your situation and why you're looking for a group," I said to her. She began to sob, telling about her brother, Lorencio, who died of AIDS last September. She wants help with the loss. She has taken refuge in drugs and has gotten into trouble with the law and is now on probation.

I listened as carefully as I could, encouraging some limited debriefing and expressing of her grief which helped me assess how at risk she was. "Tell me how you are right now," I asked, "Are you feeling like 'using' right now?" "I feel like using all the time," she said. Then she went on to say, "but I know it won't help and that I need to do something else."

She was looking for that something else. We set up an appointment for the following Tuesday morning. I expect that seemed a long time away for her. She had done extensive journaling soon after he died and she mentioned that she hadn't gone back to read any of it. I asked if she had someone she could invite over to be with her while she read her journal. She right away thought of a woman in her AA group who had offered to be her sponsor. She felt she could ask her to be with her. With that settled, I promised to mail some grief care worksheets to her that day that she could work on before next Tuesday.

I did those things and then went on with other responsibilities.

At 11:30 a.m. that same day, I was trying to leave the building to go to a four-hour meeting with some of our staff and the staff from Public Health. I encountered Ben, the client I had first met in the hospital when he was diagnosed with HIV. He was the young alcoholic who had never recovered from his mother's murder when he was nine. Ben threw his arms open toward me and then closed them around himself. "I've been drinking," he said and started to cry. We talked a few minutes and a volunteer offered to get him some food. I left for the parking lot.

Ben followed me out, more desperate than I had ever heard him, crying and expressing despair. I told him I wanted him to go to VCMC and see Waldie, his counselor. He said she would only yell at him. "That's because she cares about you and doesn't want you to do bad things to yourself. You need to go there, Ben. I'm not able to do this now. I need to leave." He had no money for the bus and I gave him a dollar in change, knowing it might not be enough incentive to get him onto the bus, but I asked him to do it for me. He went back into the building saying he loved me.

I offered the first grief support group specifically for clients. Most of our clients had experienced many losses, but for reasons I had no way of knowing, only four people showed up. Art, who was one of them, came only to the first of the six meetings because of a scheduling conflict. Having Art at the first meeting probably deluded me into thinking a group of four could be an effective group, because Art is a great group member. But then it was down to three. So for five weeks I did my best with a group that was beyond difficult to manage. One member liked talking, while another said almost nothing. Every meeting I was struggling to draw out the extremely shy member and include the third man, all while gently limiting the talkative member. I have a lot of experience in small group facilitation, but I ignored my first rule which is to have at least six participants. I can tell you I paid a price for that misjudgment. But the men did come each week and appeared to appreciate the chance to attend to their grief.

Visiting patients and conducting memorial services continued. I visited Robert in his upstairs apartment downtown. He was close to the end of his life, he told me. He asked if I would do his memorial service.

Robert's memorial service was to be held at his cousin's home. I never got comfortable conducting memorial services. It was so ingrained in me that these were something done by clergy. But clients identified me as a spiritual figure who was unequivocally there for them and they trusted that I would reflect lovingly on their lives and that I would conduct a service if asked. Many clergy declined to conduct services for people who had died of AIDS. Some others took this final opportunity to speak of the "sins" of the deceased.

My goals in approaching each service were honoring the one who had died and supporting the grieving. Meeting with family or partners of the deceased to plan the service was a valuable opportunity to be with them in their early grief process. It was a chance to talk about their loved one as we put the service together. Sometimes I would produce the bulletin myself, making it as beautiful as I could. I got to know the paper aisle at Staples very well as I labored to make beautiful memorial bulletins and other kinds of notices. If beauty is a channel of spirit, we needed beauty in the AIDS-affected community any way we could get it.

A couple of days after planning the service with Robert's cousin and her husband, and while we were still putting the finishing touches on the service to be held the next weekend, I received a letter from her:

> Thank you for all your help during this very difficult and confus-
> ing time in our lives. Last night after we all spoke and had that
> meeting I told my husband when I walked in that I felt as if the
> angels had just lifted a heavy load off of me, and that's all because

of you…I will be telling everyone at the conclusion of the service my "thank you's," and I feel that will be all I can really handle at this time without breaking down, no matter if I say what I feel or you say it for me, I know in my heart I will not be able to keep it together, and I have to in order to complete everything that Robert has asked of me. I thank you for your offer in helping me out with this matter, for being so kind to (us), but most of all for the love and understanding that you have given us at this time.

Reading her letter, my mind returned again to when I was an APLA volunteer and my first AIDS memorial service. I recall how difficult it seemed to be on Tom's partner to have to plan and conduct the service while grieving. How my heart went out to him. It had been a long road to this time, where I was in a position to help. Having been in spiritual community with people, I could accompany them to the end.

A few days after the service, Robert's partner gave me a gift made by Robert, who had been part Chumash Indian. It was a ritual bundle of feathers bound together with a seashell attached. I'm not familiar with ways of using ritual objects in the Chumash tradition. For me this ritual bundle is representative of Robert's heritage of Chumash life on the mainland and on the Channel Islands. I display it in my library, in memory of Robert.

Carrie was a non-attending Episcopalian who was participating in Spiritual Questing. Her son, Jack, was living with AIDS in Palm Springs. I never met him. When he died in August, Carrie wanted me to conduct a memorial service at her home and I agreed to do so. Her other son and two daughters arrived in town and we all sat down together to talk about the service. First I asked them to talk about Jim while I made notes. They wanted me to offer a eulogy.

When the day of the service arrived the family had done a great job setting up chairs in the garden, near a fountain Jack had installed for Carrie. Everything was beautifully arranged. A lot of friends and family came, including a group from Spiritual Questing that was there to support Carrie.

The theme of my reflection was how we might honor Jack's life by remembering his values and qualities and keeping those alive in our own lives: his generosity, exuberance for life, and care for others. I included in my remarks the suggestion that we might honor Jack's life by repairing ways that our society—and especially many churches—were continuing to avoid being in supportive ministry with people living with AIDS:

The gay community has been everywhere trying to support their own who have been living with and dying with AIDS. Jack lost many friends to AIDS. The family recalled numbers of friends who asked Jack to scatter their ashes when they were gone. And he did. We need to have more people step forward in service and ministry in the AIDS-affected community. Behind the churches' reluctance lies attitudes of nonacceptance of gay men. As we celebrate the gifts of gay men and lesbians, we will honor Jack's life and the struggles he had with homophobia. And perhaps it will fall to some of you present to help correct this attitude of nonacceptance. If it does, grasp the opportunity with joy and let Jack's exuberant and caring spirit encourage your heart.

During the reception, I heard Glen from our Spiritual Questing group say he wanted me to give his eulogy when he died. Blessedly he is very much alive as I write this. Maybe he'll speak at my funeral.

19

Spiritual Questing

Spiritual Questing continued as the heart of our chaplaincy services. One challenge was maintaining a stable group when the participants were living with an unpredictable virus. Spiritual Questing was stable through most of 1995, then deaths, illness, and moves made it rocky through the next year. Sometime around 1997, Doug and I opened the group to caregivers, with a wide definition of the word "caregiver": partners, family members, AIDS Care volunteers, and close friends were all welcome. This was a fortuitous change. Caregivers, as well as our clients, were struggling with the losses and ravages of AIDS. By '96-'97, some clients were dealing with additional issues as they realized there was now the possibility of living with the virus. Whatever their issues, clients and caregivers were seeking to find solid ground in spiritual practice and community. Most of them had not yet found this in local churches, at least in the context of their AIDS-affected lives. The caregivers helped stabilize our Spiritual Questing group.

I generally planned Spiritual Questing as a series of eight weekly meetings followed by a three-week break during which I would search for new content and approaches and would advertise the dates for the next group. Also, having a break allowed participants to leave for a while if they wished and for new people to be incorporated. The current participants seldom left unless they moved away, but new people did arrive. The longtime members were invariably welcoming to new people. Some of our members may have learned that in twelve-step groups. All I know is they were very good at it.

Coming up with good *lectio* passages and reflection questions for the weekly meetings was challenging. Initially, Norvene Vest's ten pages of passages from Scripture and religious classics published in *Bible Reading for*

93

Spiritual Growth had been my main source for passages. It was also a way for me and the group to meet some of the great spiritual writers.

I have a fond memory of Carol asking, at the conclusion of a meeting, "Can we have more passages from Jean-Pierre de Caussade?" We had read one several weeks earlier from his book *The Sacrament of the Present Moment,* written in the 1700s. I thought, if only churches could hear this, a young, unchurched woman with HIV requesting *lectio* passages from Jean-Pierre de Caussade! Probably most church members would never have heard of him. These were the moments which in memory can bring me to tears for love of these determined searchers who were finding their way to the sacred. I also was on the journey, following whatever light I had into the life I had been called toward, into this ministry to which God had summoned me.

I think it was during 1997 that, having finally exhausted Norvene's compilation of passages and worn myself out searching here and there for new passages, I finally started planning each series around a theme and drawing passages from the books of deep and quotable authors. I found books by Henri Nouwen especially valuable. Themes I worked with were trust, fear, acceptance, and prayer, among others.

Working with thematic material helped me focus my preparation for each series. It also made Spiritual Questing more responsive to core spiritual needs that people brought to the group.

Now with Doug as a co-leader, we would brainstorm about the direction for each series and, sometimes, add elements. Doug was part of an ongoing journaling group. We decided to incorporate journaling into a series on the theme of trust. He provided eight sentence completion ideas, one for each week in the series. "I remember how alone I felt when…" "If it's going to get done, I do it myself because…" "I had a strong sense of trust in myself when…" "I felt like I was following the leading of the sacred when…" "I felt included and valued when…" These and other examples were productive starters for eliciting each participant's core stories. Each person had her or his own stenographer's notebook for the series and wrote what came to mind in the reflection part of each meeting. People would share their reflections if they wished to. The sharing times were powerful. One woman shared how fearful and alone she felt when, as a teenager, she was raped and the parent at home would not comfort her. A man shared his memory of his drunk father barging into church and herding him and his mother out. On the way home his father was violent with them both.

Spiritual Questing became a setting for the search for meaning in our life stories, and for reflecting on how we each had learned to respond to the struggles life presented to us, and for thinking about our strengths and hopes. Week by week we were there respectfully hearing one another's stories and participating in a movement toward the life in God we were longing for.

One of my goals for Spiritual Questing was to offer a community where participants could feel safe speaking of challenges they were having with HIV, whether it was their own or that of a loved one, and about their spiritual lives. The other key goal was to encourage participants in their search to discern the divine reality at the source of their own lives.

An important struggle which came up for some clients in the group in '96-'97 was the challenge of staying on their meds. The medications had difficult side effects that anyone would want to avoid. However, some of this conversation was rooted, I learned later, in survivor guilt, clients feeling they didn't deserve to live when so many friends had died. I had no depth of understanding of the issue but their struggle was on my mind as a spiritual need in the group as I planned each series of meetings. The content and how God could work through the group made up for issues I did not understand. What we did together in Spiritual Questing always bent toward their belovedness, beloved by us, beloved by God.

Several times a year at the conclusion of a series, I would ask participants to respond to a questionnaire evaluating their sense of community, sense of safety, and the degree to which the program was assisting them in their spiritual journey. They were also invited to evaluate specific elements of that particular series. I would ask them to comment on experiences that stood out as positive or negative and to name anything that was assisting them in their spiritual life. Recommendations for specific program changes were always invited.

I read them carefully, taking their feedback seriously. I have kept all the evaluations. Why have I kept them? Perhaps I needed this concrete evidence that God was working through this program, and was at work through me.

Although the evaluations included critiques of the program elements, such as the journaling feature, which guided our planning, the enduring impact on me personally was their comments on the importance of Spiritual

Questing for them. Comments like, "It is my weekly church service, my only true devotional time," or "The passages have allowed me to feel precious in who I am for the first time in my life." In answer to the question of what they were finding helpful in their spiritual lives, one person wrote: "The wisdom to turn to prayer and meditation as a reliable healing process and alternative to old habits."

In response to the question of any experience that particularly stood out for them, one man wrote, "I feel that God's hand was there directing me to reach out to others." The same man also wrote that he felt accepted from the start of the series. Another man (he chose to sign it) wrote, "Pat's love and nonjudgmental personality gave me a sense of security and the ability to look at myself without fear."

Julian of Norwich, the fourteenth-century English mystic, said we are not just made by God we are made of God. The impact of Spiritual Questing was, I think, that we knew we were, to use a term from the Reverend Dr. Ed Bacon, touching the "godness" in ourselves and in each other. It was a huge breakthrough for most of our clients and, at a certain level, for me. I needed to put aside nagging questions about how I, Pat Hoffman, a laywoman with years of working in social justice movements, could now be a chaplain and be leading this program of spiritual support which people were finding important! The clients' willingness to accept my leadership allowed my own "godness" to be available, to them and to me.

In the mid-1990s, the church was still largely AWOL from the AIDS-affected community. But God had called me, a laywoman, to enlist in "God's movement of love,"[1] as Ed Bacon speaks of it. Maybe I had always been in that movement, but now, instead of getting people to take some particular action on behalf of the marginalized and those suffering (although I was still doing that in my talks in churches), I was lighting the path for people on a journey into their own souls, and they were finding God was there and always had been.

One night in Spiritual Questing, Art spoke about his past experiences in the church. "The message was," he said, "'You're broken and God isn't.' In Spiritual Questing I've discovered our unity in God that transcends whether we're broken or not. In this group the focus is off of the brokenness and on the wholeness. We're on a path toward wholeness." At that time, Art,

---

1. Bacon, Sermon preached at All Saints Episcopal Church, Pasadena, California, January 31, 2016.

who had been part of the original Spiritual Questing group which met at St. John's Medical Center, had been a "Quester" for nearly three years.

Doug asked one of the women in Spiritual Questing to write a letter to the Ventura County AIDS Partnership in support of an AIDS Care funding request for the program. Carol had been attending Spiritual Questing for ten months. She wrote, "This group has been very instrumental in helping me achieve acceptance and hope in my day to day living with HIV. It has brought balance to my life. . . . When Pat Hoffman announced an upcoming retreat I was just tickled. I attended the last retreat for Spiritual Questing. I remember it as being one of the greatest experiences of my life. I am very fond of the relationships with the other members of the group. Our sharing of memories and experiences has created such a wonderful bond. I remember coming home feeling so clean and shiny and totally renewed."

Our first small retreat, exclusively for Spiritual Questing participants, was an overnight retreat held at a big beach house just north of Ventura. Cecil and I had taken our family there years before. It was owned by a Lutheran pastor and his wife and, as I recall, they waived the usual rent for our Spiritual Questing weekend.

I invited an Episcopal priest who was also a Buddhist practitioner to spend Saturday with us, teaching us to meditate. My friend from CPE, Christina Fernandez, who was studying with the priest, joined us as well. Meditation was a new tool in the coping repertoires of most of our clients. They approached this chance to learn seriously and with eagerness.

They loved just being together in this house by the beach, sharing meals and having free time to watch the waves and hear the ocean. But even this lovely lull in their normal lives created challenges for some. I remember walking up the beach with one of the men. He shared with me that he didn't want to walk very far because his medications caused diarrhea. He always needed to know how close a bathroom was. The early "cocktails" could have a lot of side effects.

20

Retreats as a Time to Teach Belovedness

Our subsequent small, annual retreats were held in a retreat house in Montecito at La Casa de Maria. The positive experiences of retreatants from Spiritual Questing were important in reassuring reluctant clients that our larger spiritual support retreats were okay to attend. I can just imagine some gay guy receiving a retreat flier and saying, "They're holding a Spiritual Support Retreat at some Catholic-sounding retreat center? Oh yeah." But if some buddy of his had gone and liked it he might consider attending.

Leading retreats was new for me. Doug and I were planning two a year, the small one for Spiritual Questing participants (usually about a dozen men and women) and a larger one for any clients or caregivers involved with the agency. As word of mouth spread, they began to draw about thirty or more participants, and our largest had thirty-seven.

Each large retreat had an overall theme rooted in our planning committee's perception of the spiritual needs of clients (there were always one or two clients on that committee). We would pick a theme and then my daughter Mary would help us with visual elements and creative activities to express that theme. I was aware of being a word person and knew I needed creative ideas for visuals and activities.

The theme for the first retreat I worked on after being hired was loss and grief. Mary suggested having a bare stage-prop tree which we placed at a break in our circle of chairs. Mary cut out dozens of leaves, some green and others in fall colors. The first full day of this weekend retreat, we gave these leaves to retreatants and invited them to write on each of their fall leaves some loss they had experienced. After twenty minutes, a bell rang signaling them to begin writing on the green leaves what they wanted to bring back or introduce into their lives. After twenty minutes the bell rang again calling people to return to the room and to our Great Circle. (Doug was trained in the use of the Council Circle and taught it to me. In Native American cultures it was developed as a respectful, egalitarian method of sharing. Always performed in a circle, a Talking Stick or other ceremonial object is passed around the circle. Each person speaks only when they are holding that object. We used this process on every retreat.) Back in the circle, people were asked to scatter their losses at the base of the tree and hang the green leaves on the branches. The tree then, all leafy and full of life, stood as a symbol throughout the weekend. We carried the theme of accepting our losses and identifying what we can bring into our lives in each plenary, held in Council Circle.

Mary helped us again the next year when our theme was "Our Lives as Sacred Story." I bought good quality journaling books with blank covers. Mary helped us assemble piles of magazines (including back issues taken—with permission—from our family dentist's office), glue, and scissors. The first night of the retreat everyone decorated the cover of his or her journal in a way which reflected their sense of themselves. The visual focus when we gathered in the great circle was a small table with boxes of different shapes and sizes draped with fabric. On these were holy books, the Bible, the Koran, and Buddhist teachings. When retreatants had finished decorating their journaling books, they were invited to place them at that focal point with the other sacred books. Each day they would retrieve their books for directed writing exercises in small groups.

An extraordinary story came out of the small group I led. One man in the group had a slave/master relationship with his partner. Their relationship was enacted as a kind of ongoing game with the one in my small group playing the role of the slave. In his journaling he shared that he no longer wanted that role. The retreat was, apparently, an occasion for him to revalue himself. I liked both of these men and didn't want to be a party in their splitting up. But the man in my group had a chance to reflect on his life and to realize the game was no longer working for him. He needed something different in the relationship, which was an important step for him.

The night before that retreat, I called Ruth asking for help while I was working to pull all the strands together. As a marriage and family therapist, Ruth was trained in hypnotic suggestion elements which can be expressed during guided meditation. I wanted to use a meditation at the close of the retreat. Over the phone she gave me the guidelines and I wrote everything down.

Two days later, during the retreat's closing circle, I led the group in a guided meditation which encouraged them to picture in detail where and when they would journal after they returned home and how it might feel to be writing in their journals. As people were leaving, James, who came to see me in my office from time to time, came up to me and said, "I'm not going to write in this journal." I was a little startled by what seemed an unnecessary statement of resistance. I told him it was his to do with as he wished. About ten days later, he asked if he could come upstairs to see me. When he arrived he had the journaling book with him. Instead of writing in it, he explained, he was filling it with images which were meaningful to him. I was touched that he wanted me to know this and, in fact, to see what he was doing. This was a blessed moment.

In 1993, I discovered Frederick Buechner's *Now & Then: A Memoir of Vocation*[1], the memoir of his early years. In it he asserts that God speaks to us in the details of our lives and therefore we must pay attention to our lives and discover there our own sacred journeys. The book had a deep impact on me and it helped shape my thinking. A conviction that our stories are sacred and therefore worth writing and speaking of is a way of sacramental- izing our lives—every part of all of our lives.

The people AIDS Care served had been wounded, some of them deep- ly, within the communities where they grew up and by organized religion. I wanted to give them opportunities to speak about the ways in which they had been wounded as a step in their healing. If I could help them tell their stories in settings that confirmed the sacredness of the stories, I would be leveling and straightening the highway for their journey home to their true selves. This was a bedrock idea on which I was developing the chaplaincy program for our clients and those who loved them.

The third large retreat Doug and I led together had the theme "Listening for the Voice of the Sacred." This was our largest retreat. Churches had donated enough money to send thirty-seven people and every slot was filled. Mary had set us up for the opening night's activity. Tables were placed around the room laden with ribbon and other materials and glue guns. We had invited retreatants to bring any small items which had meaning for them. I had purchased small, unfinished, wooden boxes for everyone, and they

1. Buechner, *Now & Then*, 2–3.

spent an enjoyable hour and a half decorating their boxes. When finished that evening, participants were asked to place their boxes on a table, a kind of altar, set into the circle of chairs. All the decorated boxes remained there until the end of the retreat.

Throughout the weekend, the Council Circle questions encouraged participants to think about listening for the voice of the sacred in their own lives and experiences. In the closing circle they were invited to write a letter to themselves from God, the sacred, their Higher Power, the Wise One within them. (I wanted to invite in any spiritual path our people had found helpful.) Then there was a closing ritual in which each person folded the letter to themselves and placed it in the box she/he had decorated. I encouraged them to take the box home and to periodically open the box and read the letter. Right now I'm reading the message I wrote from God. I wrote it with my nondominant hand. "I'm always here with you, sometimes in the difficulties that throw you against the wall. You have to see the need for change."

Each large retreat included an educational roundtable led by Terry Monk on the latest research and advances in HIV/AIDS care and treatment. This helped empower clients in their healthcare.

I wanted the retreats to serve the whole person, so we also included an opportunity for massage. I had learned about a large network of massage therapists who offered massages to people with HIV or AIDS. Touch was important to our clients. On Saturday afternoon at each of our retreats a gentle army of massage therapists would arrive, meet their Saturday afternoon clients and then spread out across the campus to rooms or under shady trees to give massages. AIDS Care staff could sign up as well. It was there I met Nancy, who became my regular massage therapist whom I saw monthly for years. I credited her along with Dr. Patti Temple, with keeping me going physically through the demanding years.

Saturday nights on retreat we had music and dancing. On one retreat we had some folk dancing. I remember Jackson, who had done professional folk dancing, asked Art to dance. Art had danced with the corps de ballet of the Kennedy Center in Washington, DC. Seeing the two of them move was a delight. On another retreat someone had brought some Latin recordings. Latin dancing is a favorite of mine and I was pleased to have a partner or two.

I can't deny that holding an alcohol/drug-free retreat for our clients was challenging. Behaviors got out of hand at some point during each of our larger retreats. The retreat grounds are spread out and it was impossible to be aware of everything going on. Besides, Doug and I were both fairly naïve when it came to substance abuse.

One evening during a retreat, Doug and I were trying to teach the group a Sufi chant with movement and hand motions. It involved an outer and an inner circle with one circle going clockwise and the other counter-clockwise. The words were: "May the blessings of God be upon you. May God's peace abide in you. May God's spirit illuminate your heart, now and forever more." This was to be sung to each partner, with hand motions as the two circles rotated in opposite directions.

The challenge was a whole group of folks were having fits of giggling. We had no clue what was so hilarious until Art McDermott took us aside and said, "You do know what's going on? They've been down by the creek smoking marijuana." We didn't know. Some of the gigglers were Spiritual Questers and they loved us and wanted to cooperate, but they were finding it difficult. We did finally get everyone doing this little Sufi chant and dance.

On another occasion a group of people were drinking wine or beer in one of the guest rooms. It was at night after the final circle of the day so it had little impact on the retreat program; however, I did worry that La Casa staff would not welcome us back if they were aware of drug and alcohol use. I didn't want to alienate the staff which had always been great to us, very accommodating, and supportive. The retreat center is owned by the Immaculate Heart Community, a progressive women's community that had become a lay community after tangling with the pope a few decades ago.

On another occasion a gay couple were attending for the first time. We got word they were drinking hard liquor in their room in spite of the stated prohibition. Doug and I were concerned about this and I agreed to talk with the couple, privately. This was not my forte, but I went and let them know we had zero tolerance on our retreats for drugs and alcohol. It still embarrasses me to remember my "zero tolerance" speech, like we even knew what was going on during their free time, let alone having a mecha-nism for controlling it. The couple left that night. I don't know if that was a good thing or bad. I felt like matters between me and that couple were left incomplete with a distance between us.

Years later, Doug ran into James, our young client who attended that retreat. Doug mentioned how upset he had been with the couple drinking.

James looked at him and said, "That retreat changed my life." The Sacred Spirit depends on us to be doing our work and usually that work is uneven in quality. She does what she can with both our skilled and unskilled efforts.

21

The Agency in Trouble

AIDS Care had expanded to include a prevention program which Ron Spingarn was hired to direct. Sal Fuentes, who was from the area, was brought on staff to work with Ron. Much of their prevention work was with men who have sex with men (MSM), the descriptor used in minority communities where there was the highest stigma attached to a homosexual orientation. There was a growing number of women becoming infected through sex with their husbands or male partners who were also having sex with men. Homophobia was a significant factor in the rapid rise of infections in MSM communities. Prevention education was life-saving work.

Ron and Sal had their office upstairs where Doug and I were. Ron, expressing an interest in what I was doing, invited me to lunch to ask me about the chaplaincy program. His interest was a relief to me after some of the resistance I had experienced from other staff. It must have been 1996. In December of that year there was a party and staff gift exchange. I still have the note Ron included with his gift to me: "Pat, I feel like you're the guiding light for me in this world of crazy-making in which we work and live. Thanks for you serene strength. Love, Ron."

Reading it again all these years later, I've been thinking about what he saw in me as serene strength, since I don't remember feeling serene. Was I presenting a false self or did I have a faulty sense of self? In any case, Ron's friendship was, and remains, an encouragement.

AIDS funding, especially MSM funding, was always challenging. As the effectiveness of protease inhibitors became apparent, their very effectiveness became an excuse to reduce funds even though new cases of HIV were flooding into clinics, including the Immunology Clinic in Ventura. Most of the new infections were in gay men. Nonetheless, women infected by gay or bisexual men, because they were seen as innocent victims, became more of a focus of the decreasing dollars. Toward the end of 1997, both federal AIDS funding and California state office of AIDS prevention money were cut, particularly prevention money targeted at men who had sex with men. Nationally, the religious right was swaying decisions. Through their powerful influence, almost all prevention money was earmarked for school-based initiatives focused on promotion of abstinence. It would be several years before program managers could demonstrate that was a tragic mistake.

Doug tried to find other funding for our prevention program, but foundations were getting tired of AIDS, moving on to other causes. By the end of 1997, Ron and Sal were both gone, our short-lived prevention program gutted. I stayed in touch with Ron, who lived in Santa Barbara with his partner, but it was hard to not have him and Sal present on a daily basis.

We all showed up at the theater downtown to see "Rock the Boat," a documentary about an HIV-positive crew which had sailed in the Trans-Pacific race from San Pedro, California to Honolulu—a distance of 2,250 miles. Rob Hudson, our Board chairman, was part of this venture, along with Joe Rund, the attorney who did pro bono work with our clients, and John Proctor. They formed the nonprofit Get Challenged to make the film. The documentary filmmaker was Bobbi Huston.

It was a big, expensive project intended to show what people with HIV could do. No more death sentence. They were going to be out in the world living. Rob wanted AIDS Care to sign on with seed money during 1997, and Doug agreed to contribute $5,000. The crew pulled their act together, outfitted their sailboat, and did practice sails. When the starting day came they were ready and set out at a good clip. They encountered some serious weather, but made it to Honolulu. Through the course of the race, Bobbi Huston was on board filming. It was an exciting documentary and was in contention for an Academy Award.

There were a lot of personalities involved in this project and I never knew what happened, but Rob left the Board and there were some kind of interpersonal dynamics that caused Doug some angst. He definitely didn't need more pressure at that time.

The El Nino rains in January and February of 1998 mirrored the mood at AIDS Care as funding washed away. I was spending more time helping with proposals and writing reports to funders. Our mental health funding was holding up and I decided to peel off that piece of work and we brought Susan Gilles, MS, on staff to direct the mental health program. I reduced my hours to twenty per week.

Work with clients was the rainbow that kept me going. I was making regular home visits to a man who was on hospice care. His partner was our client and had asked if AIDS Care's chaplain would come for a visit. Their hospice had supplied a chaplain (the pastor at Church of Religious Science) who was paid per diem to visit patients. Something had happened and she was no longer coming.

"Clark," the patient, had been a commercial pilot. He had liked the Religious Science pastor but was willing to give me a try. When I started visiting he was well enough to meet with me in the living room. Later, when he couldn't be up much, I met with him in the bedroom. I worked with objects which had some importance to him, keepsakes and gifts, giving him opportunity to talk about their meaning for him. We explored how God's love was communicated in these objects.

On one visit I asked him what he wanted at the end of his life. He told me he wanted to be surrounded by friends. His partner had been working hard to keep people away, thinking visitors would tire him, so I suggested we have his partner join us for a conversation about what he wanted, to clear up this significant discrepancy.

I had set our next appointment in advance and was going to be coming from home that day. It was raining hard and I checked for street closures. Several streets I needed to take or to cross were closed by flooding. I saw I simply could not reach their home that day. I phoned. The partner told me he was at Clark's bedside along with several close friends. Clark was dying. I told him "I can't get there because of flooding. Please put the phone to Clark's ear so I can speak to him," which he did. I told Clark I couldn't get there because of the rain. Then in a moment when instinct took over, I said, "Remember, Clark, you're a man who has flown."

About a week later, the partner came into AIDS Care to speak with me. He said, "What did you say to Clark? As soon as you spoke to him he relaxed and died." This story has remained with me as a liminal experience.

22

Dealing with Departures

Spiritual Questing was thriving with a stable group of people who were deeply committed to their spiritual journey. But in June, Art McDermott announced he was moving to Los Angeles. Art was a three-year member of Spiritual Questing. He is a person of such spiritual depth, had been a great member of the group, and he had been the director of the AIDS Partnership, a significant funding source for us. He had been the one who obtained the mental health grant with which I was brought on staff. Besides which he and I had become personal friends. It was hard to have him leave. On his last night with Spiritual Questing, we offered a sending forth ceremony for him. He would carry our blessings with him as he left.

Spiritual Questing was his church, he had said. So now that he was leaving I was thinking about a spiritual community that might suit him. Cecil and I arranged to meet him in Los Angeles at United University Church, our former congregation. It was an inclusive and welcoming church and I thought it might be a fit for Art, and apparently it was. He joined after a brief time and later was elected a member of the church council.

At about this time, Doug surprised the staff by announcing he would be leaving as director. What a double whammy! Doug was exhausted and demoralized. Recently he and I had met for dinner. He was recalling that after Get Challenged was organized, Rob Hudson had left the AIDS Care board. The sense of distancing after Doug had gone out on a limb to support that effort was painful. This was on top of other relationship strains related to decisions made due to funding cuts.

Doug's decision to leave was a particular loss for me. He was great to work with and a special friend, and he was a wonderful co-leader in Spiritual Questing and a committed participant. Leading retreats with him had been a deep joy. We were trusted colleagues for each other. To honor him, I organized a farewell event with a gathering and potluck dinner.

I began thinking about leaving, imagining what else I might want to do. Then when I turned sixty-two in July, I took early Social Security and officially reduced my hours to eleven per week. You know how that goes, of course. This step did help AIDS Care and it gave me more time to write, but my AIDS Care hours were always more than eleven.

In September, Doug left AIDS Care and Carol Nickell came on as our new director. We liked Carol and felt hopeful about working with her.

I was still doing more hours than I had intended to. Susan Gilles, whom we had hired to take over the mental health program, was unable to continue. We hired another therapist, Paul Booth, who had taken our training and specialized in drug and alcohol issues. In September, I was spending time acquainting him with the program and strategizing with him about a fresh approach to working with clients who wanted counseling but sometimes didn't show up for appointments with our volunteer therapists.

October, as AIDS Awareness month, was always busy. I was asked to speak at a special AIDS service at California Lutheran University. I also preached at St. Paul's Episcopal Church in Ventura, which had been a reliable support church for us. My strongest memory of that day was of a man in the third pew standing up and interrupting my sermon to make some negative comment about gay men. I paused momentarily and then continued on and he sat down. After the service I tried to find him to speak with him, but without success. A few people told me how embarrassed they were by his outburst. Homophobia was a steady problem in our work.

For some people, the protease inhibitors were too late. Omar, a longtime client, died at the beginning of the month. My love for the clients helped keep me on the job. My sorrow, however, was hard to sustain. In October, I made this journal note:

> I want to find my way to Joy. I'm looking for the path. There was another death this week. Omar died Monday night within an hour of receiving the sacraments. I'm feeling too much accumulated sorrow.

Doug was still living in the area, thank God. During October there was a National AIDS Conference in Dallas. During the summer I had proposed to Doug that he and I do a workshop we would call "Retreats on a Budget." I prepared handouts on how to work with different themes and on doing outreach to churches to fund them. For Doug and me the trip was fun. We stayed at Doug's brother's home on the outskirts of Dallas. After the conference, we flew to Albuquerque where we rented a car and drove north to Ghost Ranch for a retreat led by my longtime friend, Chris Glaser, on the teacher and writer, Henri Nouwen. It was a magical week of being led and nurtured in the crisp October air of the ranch.

Doug and I still laugh about our experience traveling together. I was the one who always had extra quarters for the luggage carts and healthful travel snacks in my purse. He, on the other hand, inspired me with his care-free trust that whatever he needed would be available to him. He was an experienced traveler and, it seemed, his relaxed attitude had worked out. He did, however, appreciate the convenience of my preparations.

23

More Challenges

Sonia French, one of our two case managers, gave notice. Her doctor husband had finished his medical residency at VCMC and was taking a position in another state. Judy Higgins continued on a little longer, managing the whole case load alone. But not long after Sonia's departure, Judy also left to take a better-paid position with a well-established agency. Their departures created more instability at AIDS Care. There was only enough money to fill one of these positions.

The new case manager was Martin Perrier. Martin had left a Roman Catholic men's religious order and took on this new work with commitment. I found him easy to work with and we became friends.

As things came apart, I became more intentional planning what else I wanted to do. In my new free time I had started a weekly women's journaling group at Ventura County Community College. It was a great group of women and we met in a community room for a program for women returning to or starting college later in life.

Also, Nick Street, an editor with Westminster/John Knox Press, had contacted me about writing a book for them. I had proposed a book about Spiritual Questing. He liked the idea! I began conceptualizing the book.

Toward the end of 1998, AIDS Care lost its lease on our Palm Street house. Carol Nickell was searching for another property that would be easy for our clients to access by public transportation and could accommodate the staff. She found a two-story historic house on Thompson, still downtown.

There are always problems to be solved when an agency moves. An unusual problem we had was in our Palm Street location's garden. The ashes of two clients had been buried in that garden by people who loved them. Now the property would be leased by a business of some entirely different nature. I'm not sure what the involved family members did with those ashes. Did they move them? Did they move them to the small garden area at our new offices? This problem was emblematic of the emotional investment people had in that space.

Cecil and I were in Pasadena on December 28th, celebrating our forty-fourth wedding anniversary. Over the course of the weekend we got together for lunch with Lynn Wilson, a longtime friend. She asked about my work and was particularly interested in Spiritual Questing. Hearing the dire money woes of the agency, she offered to cover the expenses (mainly my time) for three series of Spiritual Questing in 1999. Lynn's gift assured another year of Spiritual Questing. It also helped me move into a looser relationship with AIDS Care as a contract worker.

Carol Nickell met with me to discuss my idea of working on contract. Her request was that I continue the Spiritual Questing groups, lead a 1999 retreat, and staff the October vigil, all on contract. By January, I was developing one more piece, being AIDS Care's contributed staff person one day a week at the Immunology Clinic. This was an idea I remembered from my years with the National Farm Worker Ministry. The NFWM would contribute staff to the United Farm Workers union. We sent a proposal to the AIDS Consortium requesting a grant to cover paying me to be the chaplain at the clinic one day a week. (The Immunology Clinic now ran daily with one day just for women.) AIDS Care received the grant.

I asked Doug if he would like to co-lead one more retreat with me. The February retreat would be for Spiritual Questing participants and would again be held at La Casa de Maria. He said yes without hesitation and told me that leading our retreats together had been one of his favorite pieces of work at AIDS Care.

This was our third small spiritual growth retreat. The theme was "You are the Beloved." We took our material from Henri Nouwen's books including one by that title. Participants were housed together in Casa Teresita with bedrooms upstairs and a kitchen and meeting room downstairs. We were surrounded by the beautiful grounds of La Casa, which our participants had come to know and love. One of the women said it was "where God lives." I could agree it is one of those serene places that helps us be in touch with the sacred Spirit.

Doug's apartment was near the retreat center so he went home at night. I asked La Casa for a guest room away from Casa Teresita. Being with people day and night was too wearying for me.

I remember this as a sweet retreat. There were nine participants, plus Doug and me. Art drove out from Los Angeles to attend. We all had breakfast together in the small kitchen. There were boxes of cereal out on the table and we often joked around. Art jokingly complained to Doug that I had put my hand into the cereal box. There was this re-creation of a family.

For our meetings we sat around in the living room on sofas and over-stuffed chairs working with Henri Nouwen's spiritual affirmations such as, "All I want to say to you is, 'You are the beloved,' and all I hope is that you can hear these words as spoken to you with all the tenderness and force that love can hold. My only desire is to make these words reverberate in every corner of your being."[1]

This theme was close to my heart for each person attending. It was a weekend in which we were all immersed in belovedness. If I could have done this with every client I would have.

However much I loved my ministering role, the need for my administering skills was always near. Helping raise the money for my programs was essential now to keeping them going. Putting this retreat on cost $935 of which I raised $850 from two church sources: Trinity Lutheran in Ventura, and the Roman Catholic AIDS Ministry Outreach. La Casa reduced their costs in order to help us. Nothing was easy. Yet, as we wrapped it up, I felt some sadness because I was pretty sure this would be our last retreat. With Doug's support we had been able to lead seven spiritual support retreats which invited participants into their deepest identity in God. At the time, I knew Doug's support for me was unwavering, but I didn't understand then the depth of Doug's own commitment to the spiritual lives of our clients. The sacred Spirit had led us, these two lay people in how to do this, how to guide this wounded community back toward their birthright as sons and daughters of the holy.

1. Nouwen, *Life of the Beloved*, 26.

I took March as an unpaid vacation month. AIDS Care had no money to pay me in March and I needed the time off. But it was not a carefree month. I was aware of the deaths of two clients and of the mother of a client during the month. Also, my friend Chris Glaser's mother died. She had lived in the San Fernando Valley and Chris flew out from Atlanta for the service. I drove into town and went with him to the service and then the burial.

March did give me more time for imagining my future. Nick Street, an acquisitions editor with Westminster/John Knox Press, was in Southern California and drove out to meet with me. Westminster/John Knox's interest was in a book on reaching the unchurched. I think I knew quite a bit about doing that, but it was at an inchoate level. It was like knowing how to drive to a destination but not being able to give directions to someone else. I had proposed to write the book about my experience offering Spiritual Questing to people in the HIV/AIDS community. In the coming months, I worked hard on this project, developing an outline, writing a couple of chapters, and preparing a full book proposal. Ultimately, this first proposal was a no-go. Nick liked it, but the marketing committee didn't think there would be much demand in the church for a book on how to reach the AIDS-affected community. As I was viewing the church, I thought that was probably true. I longed to write about Spiritual Questing and the remarkable, mainly unchurched people who were part of it. I couldn't step away enough to see what I instinctively understood about meeting the unchurched, de-churched, and rationally achurched. My theology was not about bringing them to church; my main mission was their discovery of God being present in them and around them. But I also wanted to bring the church to them in the sense of having the church see them for who they were as bearers of God's Spirit. Being with them was a path into the heart of the gospel, into the heart of God.

24

Looking for the Exit

I think AIDS Care moved into the new space on Thompson during March. There was an office for me, though it was understood I wouldn't be in it much. I had moved all my paper files home, but I had a desk and computer at the new offices. Martin Perrier, the case manager, was toward the back of the building where I was. Martin was great about keeping me in the loop— a real sweetheart.

When I resumed work in April, I went to the County Health office and picked up my employee badge so on the days I worked as contributed staff at the clinic it would be clear I wasn't a volunteer. I also began supervising Julie Morris, a CPE intern who joined me in clinic chaplaincy. (I'll say more about Julie later.) Since the clinic was now running several days a week, Julie took the Tuesday and I took the Wednesday women's clinic. She was a candidate for the Episcopal ministry. Dr. Prichard was pleased to have this smart, compassionate young woman covering one of the days and I the other. And none of it came out of his ever-squeezed budget.

AIDS Care was in rocky shape but Spiritual Questing was at its most vibrant. During 1999, we had our largest, most diverse group ever. Out of a dependable twelve participants they were gay, lesbian, straight, married, partnered, and single. Religiously the group was wildly diverse: a nonattending Episcopalian, the straight couple was active in a Foursquare church in town, there was an active Roman Catholic, and the lesbian couple was involved at the Church of Religious Science. The percentage of participants actively involved in church somewhere was also a notable variation from previous years.

Even with all this remarkable diversity, the people loved each other and were deeply committed to the group. It was during this year that some participants asked if they could share in facilitating the meetings. I saw this as an indication of ownership and a desire for empowerment in a process which had meant so much to them. I think four ultimately tried themselves out as facilitators.

Carol Nickell left her job as director in April or May. With the difficult funding environment, moving the offices, and all the staff changes, there was never a pause for her. I remember her saying to me, "Pat, I can do this job, but I don't want to." After Carol left there was a gap during which the Board President, Michael Masseremus, filled in as best he could. During this period, Patty Verdugo-Johnson left as our accountant/administrator. She lived in Ventura and generously made herself available for several more months to help with the transitions.

Chuck was hired as the new executive director. He lived in Santa Monica and commuted sixty-two miles each way to work. He didn't know Ventura. He had been in management at a large corporation and, as I recall, had no experience with small nonprofits. His management style was top-down. These were all red flags.

Chuck resumed our weekly staff meetings, which he held around a large dining table in a room toward the back of the house. There were usually seven or eight of us around the table. Paul Booth, our mental health coordinator, attended (his funding was secure through the calendar year), as did Martin Perrier, Mary, who was continuing part-time work with the food pantry, Adriana, who was the new administrative person responsible for bookkeeping, and Danitza, who was the volunteer coordinator who had come over from our old Palm Street offices.

I felt a lot of tension in those weekly meetings, like everyone was wary what would happen next. During the meetings I sometimes would watch Paul Booth. It seemed as though life had prepared him for this kind of experience. He was there, and he was participating, but his demeanor seemed to say, "None of this is going to ruin my day." Mary and I sat next to each other and held hands under the table. Life had not adequately prepared us for the stress we experienced in those meetings.

One morning, Chuck presented us with the agency budget in a new format. He told us that if we didn't understand our portion of the budget to feel free to come to him and he would explain it. The figures for my program were not right. I had raised the money for my program for that year and kept track of what was spent. I told him the figures were off. He, condescendingly I thought, suggested I needed help understanding the new format so we set up an appointment. It got ironed out but not during our special meeting. It wasn't until later, after he brought Patty Verdugo-Johnson in to consult with him and she told him how carefully I tracked my program budget. I found the episode aggravating and stressful.

I don't remember how it had come about for me to be asked to supervise Julie Morris, the Episcopal seminarian. Julie had done her CPE in Oxnard (where I had finished up) and wanted to have a nine-month internship in AIDS ministry. She was brought on as a chaplain intern at AIDS Care and was our person at the clinic on Tuesdays. She was willing to take on other staff duties as well.

In July, I convened the vigil-planning committee and introduced Julie, who had agreed to chair the committee. We were again planning a vigil for Ventura at Church of Religious Science and, for a second year, one in east county, to be offered in the chapel at California Lutheran University. It was the year we had our most support from churches. Two churches sponsored and planned the post-vigil receptions, and local clergy participated in a caregiver blessing at each vigil. Churches and two regional religious organizations carried our bulletin announcements of the vigil as well as the Walk for Life which was coming up later in October. St. Paul's Episcopal in Ventura, with their long history of support, donated the money for mailings related to the two vigils.

Jackson Wheeler, whose brother had died of AIDS four years earlier, served on the planning committee. Jackson remembered organizing the very first vigil in 1986. He recalled sending a letter to 100 area churches for support and not a single one responded with help. In the intervening years there had been movement and changes in attitudes toward AIDS. The response we had in 1999 was also the result of steady, persistent organizing. It helped that this was part of my job and I had the title of chaplain, which was easier for churches to relate to. And it helped that I had learned to do church organizing during the years I spent working with the National Farm Worker Ministry, organizing church support for another initially unpopular cause: supporting the strikes and boycotts of poor people who were farmworkers. Here was the method I used, in case you might want to know: you let churches know what help is needed, give them choices as to how they can assist, look for a person in the organization who cares about your cause who can be your contact, keep track of key names and contact information, thank them when they help, keep coming back, and know you are offering the institutional church entry to blessed ground.

25

Leaving Time

I knew I would finally leave AIDS Care at the end of the year, though I had funding through the following March. Yet even with all the agency's disruptions, it was difficult. How do you leave work to which you were summoned, and which has changed the configurations of your life? I needed help. I contacted a nun at St. Catherine's, a retirement community for Sisters of the Holy Cross, and asked if she could do some spiritual direction with me to assist me in saying goodbye to this ministry. She told me there was a priest in residence who was quite skilled in spiritual direction and she could arrange for him to work with me a time or two. He agreed to do so and met with me at St. Catherine's. He gave me an assignment to write a dialogue with my job. I wrote it in two parts:

October 6, 1999

Me: Well, I'm saying good-bye to you, friend. Five years ago I helped discover you, and in the process, discovered myself as a chaplain.

Job: Thank you for bringing me to light. I'm recognized now throughout the AIDS-affected community, and by the funders, as a legitimate and needed work. You've legitimized me!

Me: I brought my best to that effort. Thank you.

Job: And now the new Director wants your help in shaping what will happen with me in the future when someone else has me.

Me: It's hard for me to let go of you even though I'm tired and feel it's time to move on.

Job: You and I will always be together in some way. I'll always be in your heart. You'll carry away all that you've learned from me. And do you realize how much you've grown spiritually on this job?!

Me: Yes, I have you to thank for that. You've been a channel for the Sacred with every difficulty and challenge. Let's meet again tomorrow and discuss this further. I have a lot more inner work to do before my last day comes.

October 13, 1999

Me: Well, tonight is my final meeting with the Spiritual Questing group. For five years I've been offering this. It's the programming piece I'm proudest of. I have some ego wrapped up in this.

Job: You've done good work with Spiritual Questing. Rest in joy that you saw a need, experienced a way to meet that need, and took the risk to offer it.

Me: Thank you. I'll work on that.

In addition to some brief spiritual direction (my recollection is the priest was leaving St. Catherine's a day or two after that second entry), I was continuing to lay the groundwork for transition, including accepting invitations to lead retreats.

In early November, I took the training for national certification in bereavement facilitation. I was developing a plan to offer individual grief care in my home.

Buena Park, where the four-day grief care certification training took place, was eighty-seven miles from home in Ventura. It felt like a continent away to me. I have two strong recollections from the training: first, I passed the tests at the end of each day's presentations, and second, when I would return to my room at the end of each day I felt I might fall apart.

What was happening? Perhaps the recent stress and changes had overburdened my sense of self, and being away from Cecil, home, and family was too much. Being alone for the night in that barren hotel room gave me little to remind me of who I was. So I would phone Cecil on the room phone (before cell phones were common). Hearing his voice and talking with him about the day stabilized me. It concerned me that after all the inner work

I'd done I could lose myself in a hotel room. I felt comforted, however, that during the day, while I was in active learning mode, I was fine.

I had been taking some continuing education classes in grief care over the past five years. With thirty more hours of training, I was certified for this work.

I prepared my resignation letter and gave it to Chuck. It was set that Julie Morris would be AIDS Care's chaplain after I left at the end of 1999 and would continue for AIDS Care at the clinic. She also agreed to facilitate Spiritual Questing for the winter session of 2000. It pleased me that both of the programs I had developed, the mental health program and the spiritual support program, were staffed, funded, and would continue after my departure. I agreed to supervise Julie on a volunteer basis through her nine-month internship. I enjoyed working with her.

I wrote a farewell to our clients for the agency newsletter:

> I'm leaving my position as Chaplain effective December 12th. I want to thank the many clients I have known over these years for the opportunity to share in your personal journeys. It has been a privilege to be AIDS Care's first Chaplain and to develop a Spiritual and Emotional Support Program to serve you as clients and those who love you...
>
> Norbert, a Benedictine monk, wrote: "I have something to say to you, you who have become a part of the fabric of my life...There is an energy in us which makes things happen. When the time of our particular sunset comes, our accomplishments won't really matter a great deal, but the clarity and care with which we have loved others will speak with vitality of the great gift of life we have been for each other."
>
> You have been a gift in my life.

When Martin Perrier saw this, he said to me, "You used a quote from Norbert!"

My journal notes capture how I was feeling as my time at AIDS Care drew to a close:

> *Dec. 4*
>
> Tomorrow begins my last week of employment at ACI. It seems to me unlikely that I will ever be employed again.

Dec. 6

This afternoon will be my last time at the clinic. I approach it with a sense of relief. In the four years I have been at the clinic I've had to put myself forward so much to connect with people. I feel worn out by it. But I feel I've been faithful and done my best with the clients in this new field of outpatient chaplaincy.

Dec. 13

As of this morning I'm no longer employed at AIDS Care. I have a feeling of relief that I will have little need to interact in the future with the director. I will probably miss the identity of being a chaplain who works somewhere. I may miss the sense of meaning I have had on my job. I will continue to have contact with several clients. Time will reveal how that will work out.

I feel interest and energy about the new endeavors I am planning. The waiting of this Advent season is a good theme for now.

Dec. 14

"Yesterday I turned in my key, with a feeling of reluctance. It symbolized for me loss of access, and loss of belonging.

All through the day I was wanting to check systems to see if anyone had tried to reach me, but I have no office voice mail now and I've turned off my personal pager. I went to my new Post Office box, but nothing was in it.

Dec. 28—Our 45th wedding anniversary

Forty-five years ago on the 28th I could not have imagined my life all these years later. It's not that my life is so surprising, but that I was so engulfed in being nineteen and getting married so that day – that time – seemed to be everything.

January 8, 2000

This past week I felt glad the holidays were over and I could begin this new phase of my life in which I'm not employed. I did a limited amount of work on the new book and preparing to lead a retreat in March. I invested quite a chunk of time and thought into a Farewell AIDS Care is giving for me, mainly who to invite and worrying about that, especially since everyone will need to pay for their own dinner. I did some good work in clearing up some piles of old mail, mostly newsletters and catalogues. I want a serene home and work space.

The farewell dinner for me was at the end of December with thirty or forty people, mostly clients and family members. Art McDermott had driven out from Los Angeles to be the MC. He spoke about me first, and then opened the floor for others. It was moving to hear what had been important to people: to feel valued; to be able to express a full range of feelings including anger; to be themselves; to have someone see the good in them; to be presented a broad view of the sacred.

I held all this in my heart with gratitude and with hope that I could continue to find ways to offer these gifts.

At the farewell dinner, we sat at round tables for eight. I sat with Cecil, Ruth and Bruce, my good friend Dorothy Scovil, MFT, who had taken over the counseling program I had started, my dear friend Dr. Patty Temple, who volunteered with our clients and had become my chiropractor, her partner Miki, and my friend Carol, who was part of Spiritual Questing. You couldn't have that particular group together without having fun and laughter.

Having Art McDermott come out from Los Angeles to be the MC was heartwarming. He is so good at that kind of thing and we had become close friends, as we are to this day. I missed Doug's presence. He was living in Boston at this time. Women from the family support group came for the occasion as well as some former staff. I was particularly touched that Sal Fuentes came—and spoke. He was a longtime resident in the area. Sal had been on our staff until prevention money ran out. When he spoke that night, his affirmations touched me.

Mary had a major conflict that night and couldn't be there. She sent her remarks to be read.

> Since I cannot attend the dinner in honor of my mother I thought at least I could pass on my words to her in writing…Many of you who know me will say in passing, "Say hello to your mother, she is so wonderful," I always respond the same with "I know, I have the honor of being her daughter." I am told often how she has been there for people in deep and meaningful ways. My mother is sacred to me for so many reasons but her journey has altered my own as it has most of yours. We all have been touched in some profound way because she chose to say yes to her own inner calling. For this and for her I am eternally grateful.

Within days of the farewell dinner I was hearing rumors of secret plans to close AIDS Care. This was an agency started by people in the community, and supported by the community; if they were running out of money, why weren't they turning to the community to lay out the size of the problem? During the month the news became official, AIDS Care would close in March. I attended a meeting where closing and transition plans were discussed. Edie Brown, director of the Rainbow Alliance, said her organization would take over existing contracts for client services, which would be offered by an allied program they would call AIDS Project Ventura County. She wanted to be sensitive to clients who were not gay and might not want to get services from a gay organization. (In truth, AIDS Care was about as gay an organization as you could find, but that wasn't identified in the name.) The mental health program would continue with an existing grant and be staffed by Dorothy Scovil. Martin Perrier would join the new staff, continuing his work as case manager. Some of his responsibilities were covered under an existing contract. Mary was asked to continue as food pantry coordinator, but she decided to look for other work. Our 150 clients would be notified and asked if they wanted to become clients of the new AIDS Project Ventura County. I believe most made the transfer. (APVC continued to serve clients for ten more years.)

On March 10, 2000, AIDS Care closed. It was a food pantry day and Mary distributed food before she locked the door. She was the last staff person working. She joined me at noon as we gathered with a circle of clients and volunteers behind the house in the parking lot. We held hands and I led them in a prayer:

> *Come Sacred Spirit and be present in this ending that we might feel comforted in the loss.*
>
> *Free our hearts with gratitude for what has been good.*
>
> *Fill us with confidence that you will be present with us in all the endings and beginnings of our lives. Amen.*

26

"You Gotta Keep Movin' it on"

I was busy. I was busy being unemployed and trying to keep something going from my training, and from the work which had meant so much to me. Maybe I was too busy to just sit with what it had meant. Or maybe it was too soon for me to understand. I needed time to absorb, time for dreams, time for memories to teach me. I needed time to know what the past decade had been about for me.

I was working on a revised book proposal for Westminster/John Knox, which was to be a how-to book for the church about offering Spiritual Questing and giving examples from the AIDS Care groups. I wanted to share about the people who had been part of it, how remarkable they were, and, frankly, how much deeper they had been willing to go than many traditionally churched people, in my observation.

While working on the proposal, I sent out an invitation to every Spiritual Quester for whom I had an address. Twelve showed up in my living room to talk about where they were now in their journeys. I was pleased to learn that all but two had found spiritual community in various local churches. Before they left that evening I told them about the book idea and then gave them a final evaluation form with lots of room for comments. I got a one hundred percent return from them! I added this valuable material to evaluations I had filed away over the five years along with every *lectio* passage used, every reflection question, every theme developed, labeled by season and year. I had lots of material to work with and loved crediting those I had learned from, most notably the Vests, from whom I had learned the group *lectio* process.

I delivered this book proposal to Westminster/John Knox with a couple of completed chapters. The Reverend Dr. Walt Dilg, pastor of the church I attended, had been one of my readers. He had asked me, "What did you bring to this program, Pat?" It was a question I could not yet answer. It was hard for me to see my own contributions to the work I was writing about. The how-to book proposal didn't fly.

I had a chance to see Chris Glaser at the Presbyterian General Assembly in Long Beach and told him the news. He was, of course, sympathetic. Then he asked me, "Do you think you're ready to write this book?" I don't think I was. The call for me was to reflect, not on one program, but on where God's summons had taken me.

As I settled into my new, quieter life, a small private practice in grief care took shape that gave me the chance to use my training and experience in that area. I sent a letter to all the psychotherapists I had worked with, letting them know about my grief care practice. Several therapists made referrals to me. In fact, one therapist had two or three sessions with me after a parent died. The response from therapists was especially confirming. The work with clients went well. I saw grieving people experience change that helped them move on in their lives.

In March, Marianne and Dee asked me to do a memorial service for Marianne's former partner Carol's mother. Carol had died a few years earlier leaving her mother daughterless. Marianne and Dee's was a beautiful story of fidelity to this woman.

Marianne was one of the therapists who volunteered with our mental health program. We had gotten to know each other in service to the AIDS-affected community. I was glad Marianne and Dee would ask me to work on the service and I was honored to do it.

Then in the summer the phlebotomist at the clinic called. His mother had died. He and his brother wanted me to do a graveside service.

My friend and former colleague, Ron Spingarn, phoned. He and his longtime partner wanted a union service. Would I officiate? Art McDermott was in love with Jim White in Los Angeles (not the Jim White from Long Beach), and they wanted a union service at United University Church. Would Cecil and I officiate together? Yes, Yes, Yes.

I'm thinking of the Norbert quote I included in my farewell to clients:

You who have become a part of the fabric of my life. . . . There is an energy in us which makes things happen. When the time of our particular sunset comes, our accomplishments won't really matter a great deal, but the clarity and care with which we have loved others will speak with vitality of the great gift of life we have been for each other."

The job at AIDS Care was over, and in fact AIDS Care was over, but the fabric woven together out of all those relationships was whole.

One morning I had a phone call from Anne Moore, the director of Livingston Hospice in Ventura. She was needing to fill their position of staff chaplain and wanted to know if I would be interested in applying. She and I had never met, but one of her hospice nurses had suggested me. That nurse sat on an area committee I had been on which coordinated AIDS funding. Anne was looking for a trained chaplain who understood how to provide spiritual support for patients that was respectful of each person's path. She herself was an observant Jew and understood the importance of a chaplain having a spirit of inclusivity.

I was hired as their staff chaplain. I was with them in different capacities for seven years. An opportunity to work again as a chaplain! It was very different work from AIDS ministry. Patients were frequently referred for hospice care when they were already close to death. Probably 90 percent of my chaplaincy encounters were brief, often a single visit before the person died. In those circumstances the patient sometimes was no longer even able to communicate. But when we can meet one another, when as patient, family, and chaplain we all recognize the circumstances are essentially out of our control, that is graced work. That's when cracks appear in our control armor, allowing the sacred spirit access and egress.

27

The Value-Added Self

Have you ever ridden the subway in New York City or Washington, DC? You get a ticket and then load on the amount you expect to need for the trip you're taking that day. However, at some point in your day you may try to go through a turnstile and the ticket will come back to you with the message, "Add value." Then you'll need to go to a machine and put more money on your ticket.

My calling was to be a turnstile on other people's journeys, where their tickets never needed value added. My message was, "Your ticket has all the value it will ever need. Take your journey."

Communicating that message is not complicated. When we listen carefully to another person, we honor them with that attention; we communicate that we value them. This is spiritual nurture.

I'm remembering when I was a kid, especially when I was about thirteen and my sister had left and gotten married, the feeling of dining alone. Mom and Dad would come home from work. Mom would get dinner on the table (she didn't want me cooking). Then the three of us would sit down to eat. Mother and Dad would carry on an animated conversation with each other about people they encountered that day. They didn't inquire about my day, my friends, my studies. This primary setting was the place where I felt invisible.

Unfortunately, I learned in certain ways to make myself invisible wherever I was and sometimes felt hurt when people did not seem to see or hear me. I was bold in speaking up for others, but wary of speaking about myself. In my early years as a writer, I rarely mentioned myself in writing. A professional at a writers' conference finally lambasted me for that.

Years later, when my mother was in her late eighties (and still bright and sociable), she and I were visiting after dinner at our house. It was just her and me. I asked her what kind of child I had been. She fell silent, trying to remember, then said, "You never fussed." That was it. What is the opposite of spiritual nurture?

The other message was more subtle and more devastating. At an unconscious level I expected to be punished if my parents found I was acting on that which my heart led me to do. It started, I'm sure, before I was old enough to create memories of it, except perhaps in my body. My parents, along with my Dad's band, went on the road with my sister and me when I was one, just a baby, just learning to walk. Mother liked to brag that she had me toilet-trained by one. Of course she didn't want to be bothered with dirty diapers back when there were only cloth ones. But what was the price of that battle of wills, a battle I lost?

That was the prelude. During the years of travel, spending days in the car, Dad was firmly in control of when we stopped, when we ate. And I didn't fuss, apparently. Whatever happened in those years between my older sister and our parents, I don't know. I do remember Dad, furious, throwing her violently onto the bed. I do remember what seemed like a thousand dramatic scenes with my mother yelling at Martha over some infraction that never seemed like much to me.

And I remember as a teenager never having an argument with my parents. Isn't that a sure sign that something was seriously amiss?

What we most lavishly offer as adults may be what we most deeply missed growing up. I've had a passion for listening to people's stories and creating safe spaces for people to share from the hidden places of their souls. It's a blessing when what we have missed can be transformed by the Spirit into a gift we can offer.

My parents had difficulty seeing me. Maybe the Spirit worked with that, deepening my desire to see people I was meeting in the AIDS-affected community, their suffering but also their humor, and their capacities for the spiritual journey. The Reverend Dr. Walt Dilg had asked me what I brought to Spiritual Questing. I had simply used a process I learned from others, adapting it for this community, but more than that I committed to that community, seeing the deep desire of people for the journey into their belovedness.

When I came to AIDS Care to develop this first-of-its-kind program to serve HIV/AIDS clients and those who loved them, Doug's affirmation helped keep me steady. He and the clients helped me believe I could be a chaplain in their midst. They were God's angels holding me up through all the difficulties right through to AIDS Care's closure.

Back when I was a volunteer with AIDS Project Los Angeles and I asked Mark if there was anything he wanted me to do for him before I left, he told me, "No, just be you." God was speaking a word to me then: "That time is over. You can come out of hiding." It's no wonder I admired gay men and lesbians who had "come out," revealing deep and intimate information about themselves. They were a model for me.

Psychotherapist Carl Rogers wrote, "What I am is good enough, if only I can be it openly. When I am up against a difficult situation, what I am inside is good enough to meet that situation if only I would be it openly."[1] I included this quote in my art project at the end of my second unit of chaplaincy training. I knew it held significance for me. How much significance, though, I was yet to understand.

One evening, Cecil and I were watching the 2016 Democratic National Convention, with all its political speeches. Dropped into the middle of one evening, someone introduced Paul Simon singing "Bridge Over Troubled Waters." That whole, huge convention dropped their "Bernie" or "Hillary" promotions and were swaying and singing with him, carried to a heart place. I stopped eating the dinner on my TV tray. When he got to the third verse, "Sail on silver girl," I was a little embarrassed to need a tissue because I was crying.

It had been a few weeks since then. That song kept running through my mind, saying to me, "Pay attention. I'm trying to tell you something." Then one morning, thinking about the song, I googled the title and found the song came out in 1970, the year I turned thirty-five, the year all three kids were in school full-day, the year I started working for the Farm Worker Ministry. I remember wanting to be a bridge over troubled waters. That year I crafted an art piece to hang on our dining room wall. It was big, and made with a lightweight board about seventy-two inches wide and maybe

1. Rogers. *On Becoming a Person*, 51.

twenty inches high, which I covered with yellow burlap. I laboriously cut out green letters from felt which I glued onto the burlap to spell out "A Bridge Over Troubled Waters." Honest to God. That was our dining room art for years, before I replaced it with a fabulous batiked rooster. In 1970, the "Sail on silver girl" verse spoke to me. I felt that was me, a late starter, a woman who had not yet finished my bachelor's degree, but was working in this exciting job at something that could make a difference for farmworkers. But the verses evoking the image of a bridge over troubled waters were the important ones for me at that time, the words about doing for others. Standing on picket lines, going toe to toe with strike-breaking goons, traveling to distant cities to organize people, boycotting in front of stores—these activities didn't use my favorite skill sets, but wow, what opportunities to serve and to work with a movement of the poor for justice!

In the 1970s, Cecil and I had to struggle as our relationship was strained by my demanding, unconventional job.[2] Every out-of-town trip was followed by a period of hostility from Cecil. He loved what I was doing, but not my doing it. This wasn't the wife's role he had had in mind. I was anxious and pained trying to live the life I felt myself drawn to live and not have it validated by my husband, just as earlier self-determination had not been validated by my parents. Cecil and I worked this through, but it was difficult.

Fast forward to a morning in October 1992. We had moved to Ventura and I had just started clinical pastoral education at UCLA, but on this morning Cecil and I were both at home. He had put on Paul Simon's CD *Music in the Park*. I was listening to it inattentively. When it got into the tenth track, though, I woke up. It was "Bridge Over Troubled Water," and I heard that third verse, the sail on silver girl one. Hearing it took me back into a dream I had had three years earlier that I had not written down. Why not? Was it too beautiful? Was it too far out of step with what my brain had learned was my place in life? My unconscious had brought me my own, personalized "Sail On" dream, with musical accompaniment. Here's the dream:

---

2. Collins, *When Everything Changed*, 18–19. Gail Collins, writing about attitudes toward women traveling alone in the 1960s and into the 1970s, comments, "there had always been a presumption that a proper woman didn't move around too much, and there was certainly a conviction that sending a woman on a business trip raised far too many risks of impropriety."

It is night at the seashore, calm, starlit. I am rowing a small boat, sitting in the middle with two other female figures. Maybe my mother and sister. Maybe my daughters. I am rowing without effort. We sail across the starlit sea to the sound of a lullaby, "Sail baby sail, far across the sea," and arrive in China. It is still night. There are red lanterns at the dock giving us a gentle welcome. A few people are present, indistinctly, going about their business. We are going to disembark. All is ease, beauty, and welcome.

Our psyches are full of imagination. They craft amazing dreams to tell us truths when we begin to be open to those truths. I had loved that dream, talked about it with Cecil, and traced down the lullaby, which I had never sung, nor had it been sung to me. My sister-in-law, Nancy, knew it and gave me the words. Perhaps I had heard my mother-in-law sing it to one of our babies: "Sail baby sail, out upon the sea. Only don't forget to sail back again to me."[3] The permission to venture, the assurance that the parent will be waiting happily when you return from your adventure—it was a simple building block that I had missed, but I didn't write the dream down. Perhaps I couldn't incorporate yet that I could venture with ease, and without the anxiety of rejection.

When I began my journey toward AIDS ministry, those around me let me be myself with them, an unconventional woman with an unconventional call. I had been summoned to take up this work and my call was certified by gay men and women in the AIDS-affected community who welcomed me to do my work with the fullness of who I was, with the limits to what I knew, with a passion which came out of losses and propelled my heart. They taught me that just as I could see the "godness" in them, they experienced the "godness" in me.

We were traveling together into our belovedness. Thanks be to God.

3. Lyric written by Alice Riley.

The How-to of Spiritual Questing

For Those Who Want to Try it

Group Size and Makeup

A group of not less than six and not more than twelve works well. The group may be homogeneous, but the process can work well with a non-homogeneous group (e.g. male and female, gay and nongay, different religious backgrounds or lack thereof, and varying adult ages).

Length of Series

Eight weeks of once-a-week meetings works well for having a group gel as a community and for it to feel long enough for the participants to have a sense of completion. The Spiritual Questing model has appeal for people who may or may not see themselves as religious, but are searching for spiritual sustenance. People are often willing to try something for a few weeks.

Meeting Place

The location should provide quiet and privacy for the hour-and-a-half gatherings. Meeting in the same place for the eight-week series helps if someone does not attend once or twice. They will know with certainty where to go when they return.

Preparation for the Series

Identify a location where seating can be in a circle around a small table. Plan a simple worship center for the table with a cloth or runner, a Christ candle, and as many votive candles as expected participants.

Getting Started

Have a welcoming environment.
Have self-introductions around the circle.
Explain the ground rules.

1. Confidentiality: participants will not discuss what has been shared by others.

2. No cross-talk: during the meeting, participants will not comment on someone else's sharing nor make suggestions to them.

Briefly describe what the group will be doing.
Do the whole process the first meeting so participants know what to expect.

Gathering for Spiritual Questing

Process:

Gathering in Sacred Space
Sharing Joys and Sorrows
The Reflection Question
Group *Lectio Divina*
Passing God's Peace

Gathering our Real Lives in Sacred Space

The facilitator creates the atmosphere that guides participants toward bringing their real lives into the Spiritual Questing circle. There are several steps for this. They are easy but important.

1. The meeting space should be prepared with seating in a circle around a central focus, which can be on a coffee table or other low surface.

I often start with a woven runner and then place a column candle on it surrounded by votive candles, as many as there are participants expected. This visual focus announces that a normally secular area is now prepared for sacred use.

2. At the first meeting, welcome the participants to Spiritual Questing and briefly review what you will be doing and *that participants will be invited to share but always have the option to pass.* Then the importance of confidentiality should be spelled out. I usually mention that people may want to repeat other people's stories in a spirit of kindness, but to please not do so. Everyone's story is their own for only them to share. To create a sense of safety for authenticity we must respect confidentiality.

3. The facilitator invites participants to introduce themselves with whatever information seems most appropriate in your setting. Keeping this fairly brief is important so there is sufficient time for all the elements to be included in this first gathering.

Sharing Joys and Sorrows

Invite sharing of joys or sorrows. Ask participants with something they wish to share to take light from the Christ candle and light one votive candle before sharing. This symbolizes putting an experience from their lives into sacred space.

The Weekly Reflection Question

The idea of including a reflection question in each meeting of Spiritual Questing came from Elizabeth Cook, one of my supervisors when I was training for chaplaincy. I was going to be offering a Spiritual Questing group as my advanced project. Liz had been a nun and she recalled liking the reflection questions they used in community. So I tried it and continued using it in my ministry. It became a favorite feature for many participants.

Each week I would bring enough copies of the question for the next week to give one to each participant. I printed them out on a good-quality, light blue paper with some weight and texture to it. Participants liked having these questions. One man called it "taking the circle home." Another person said he taped it to his bathroom mirror as a way of keeping the question before him.

When I first began, I was conscious of the need for us all to get to know each other in terms of our spiritual lives. With a brand new group the first question might be "What name do you have for God?" Sometimes I would use, "As you find yourself in this circle what do you most want from Spiritual Questing?"

After a year or two of offering Spiritual Questing, I began planning each eight-week series around a theme such as gratitude, forgiveness, or spiritual practices. I then used reflection questions which helped participants consider their lives in terms of the theme, such as, "For what are you most grateful today?"

As the facilitator, you can open this part of the meeting by asking if someone will read the question. Then you can offer to begin. The facilitator needs to be a full participant. By going first, you can model authentic sharing of an appropriate length. Some sample reflection questions are included at the conclusion on this description of the weekly process.

Group *Lectio Divina*

I learned this group approach to *lectio divina* at a weekend retreat taught by Episcopalians Norvene Vest, PhD, Reverend Doug Vest, and a Benedictine friend, Father Luke Dysinger of St. Andrews Abbey at Valyermo, California. They had developed the method and Dr. Vest, who is seminary trained, has written the book explaining the method. I loved group *lectio divina* from the very start, finding in it a personally empowering way for people to wait on God's word to them and to discern God's call in that word.

The basic method is simple and I'm offering it here with permission from Dr. Vest, with only slight revisions to her wording.[1]

Begin by becoming relaxed and quiet.
Gently remind participants that they may pass at any time.

Listening for the Gentle Touch of the Sacred

1. One person will read aloud (twice) the passage, while others are attentive to some word or phrase that attracts them.

---

1. Vest, *Gathered in the Word*, 10. See her book for a full discussion of this process and for assistance in selecting passages.

2. Silence for 1–2 minutes. Each hears and silently repeats a word or phrase that attracts.

3. Invite participants to share aloud the word or phrase which has attracted each person. Ask them to do this without elaboration.

How the Passage Touches Me

4. Participants are invited to reflect on "Where does the content of this reading touch my life today?" while another person reads the passage.

5. Silence for 2–3 minutes.

6. Participants are invited to share aloud briefly how the word or phrase speaks to each one.

What Invitation do I Sense from this Word or Phrase?

7. Have a third reading by a third person, first inviting participants to listen for "an invitation or call of the sacred to me in this word or phrase."

8. Silence for 2–3 minutes.

9. Sharing aloud at somewhat greater length the results of each one's reflection. (Be especially aware of what is shared by the person to your left.)

10. After full sharing, pray for the person to your left. Anyone may pray silently, just stating so aloud and then saying Amen when finished. Invite group to say Amen after each prayer as a way of making it a prayer of the group.

Passing God's Peace

Offering people who have been unchurched an opportunity to pass God's peace can be deeply meaningful. It's a sacred act and a time for communal bonding, for people touching one another. When I began my work as a chaplain in AIDS Ministry in the early nineties, I was acutely aware that many in the AIDS-affected community had had experiences of people not wanting to touch them. So, for them in particular, this sacramental touching, taking of one another's hands, or embracing, was a blessing.

Conveying to participants that this is a "passing of God's peace," although certainly not to be belabored, is a subtle communication that God's peace is available within them to pass along, and to be received from others. The now popular Hindu practice of bowing with one's hands together and saying *namaste*, is similar. It means "the God in me greets the God in you." Our Christian practice is often shortened to "Passing the Peace." We can reinvest its meaning by calling it "Passing God's Peace," which is a richer symbolic act.

Before the Circle Disperses

Before participants disperse, pass out the reflection question for the next week.

When Concluding a Series

At the end of the concluding meeting in a series you might consider sending a votive candle home with each participant. That candle can represent God's Spirit coming home to dwell in their home or work space, that light always present to them.

Sample Reflection Questions

Our clients especially loved the reflection questions. I'm offering some questions we used which you may find suitable for groups you are leading.

What name do you give to that which you believe to be sacred?

What spiritual help do you hope to find in this group?

What experience(s) from your childhood or adult life were painful or hurtful and have been most difficult for you to forgive?

What in your life has encouraged hope?

For what are you most grateful today?

What do you find most often blocks your being able to feel joy and gratitude in the moment?

What do you find most often encourages your sense of hope?

What events or losses (experienced or anticipated) most challenge your sense of hope?

Is there something currently that gives your life meaning and purpose?

In what circumstances are you most likely to feel bad about yourself, to feel shame or unworthiness? Is there an example from this past week?

What is your experience if you think about the sacred present in yourself? Is that difficult or does it seem natural?

At what times in your life have you felt/do you feel the presence of the sacred?

Note: For suggested resources and sample passages with reflection questions you may email: info@spiritualquesting.com.

Bibliography

Bacon, Ed. Sermon preached at All Saints Episcopal Church, Pasadena, CA. January 31, 2016.

Buechner, Frederick. *Now & Then: A Memoir of Vocation.* San Francisco: HarperSanFrancisco, 1983.

Collins, Gail. *When Everything Changed.* New York: Little, Brown, 2009.

Frankl, Victor. *Man's Search for Meaning.* Boston: Beacon, 1946.

Hoffman, Pat. *Ministry of the Dispossessed: Learning from the Farm Worker Movement.* Los Angeles: Wallace, 1987.

———. *AIDS and the Sleeping Church.* Grand Rapids: Eerdmans, 1995.

Jung, C. G. *Memories, Dreams, and Reflections.* New York: Random House, 1963.

Newell, John Philip. *Listening for the Heartbeat of God: A Celtic Spirituality.* Mahwah, NJ: Paulist, 1997.

Nouwen, Henri. *Life of the Beloved.* New York: Crossroad, 1993.

Rogers, Carl R. *On Becoming a Person.* 1st ed. New York: Houghton Mifflin, 1961.

The Sarum Primer. Salisbury, UK: Cathedral and Diocese of Salisbury, 1514.

Tilleraas, Perry. *Spiritual Response to AIDS—The Twelve Steps.* Center City, MN: Hazelden, 1990.

Vest, Norvene. *Gathered in the Word.* Nashville: Upper Room, 1997.

"World Council of Churches Executive Committee Statement." Reykjavik, Iceland. September 15–19, 1986.